Chronicles of a Single *Mama*

Vol. 1

EVONN FIRMS

Copyright © 2019 Evonn Firms.

All rights reserved. No part of this publication may be reproduced, distributed, or transmitted in any form or by any means, including photocopying, recording, or other electronic or mechanical methods, without the prior written permission of the publisher, except in the case of brief quotations embodied in critical reviews and certain other noncommercial uses permitted by copyright law. For permission requests, write to the publisher, addressed "Attention: Permissions Coordinator," at the address below.

www.thelatterrainmovement@gmail.com – Author Evonn Firms

www.jesuscoffeeandprayer@gmail.com – Publishing House

Scriptures marked NIV are taken from the NEW INTERNATIONAL VERSION (NIV): Scripture taken from THE HOLY BIBLE, NEW INTERNATIONAL VERSION ®. Copyright© 1973, 1978, 1984, 2011 by Biblica, Inc.™. Used by permission of Zondervan

Scriptures marked NKJV are taken from the NEW KING JAMES VERSION (NKJV): Scripture taken from the NEW KING JAMES VERSION®. Copyright© 1982 by Thomas Nelson, Inc. Used by permission. All rights reserved

ISBN: 978-0-9998188-2-4

Photographer: KJ Firms

Publisher/Editor:
Jesus, Coffee, and Prayer Christian Publishing House
P.O box 691204
Charlotte, NC 28227
www.jesuscoffeeandprayer.com

Table of Contents

Foreword	vii
Acknowledgments	ix
The Definition of a Real Single Mama	1
Real Talk	1
I Had to Go Here	3
GHAMS (Gotta Have A Man Syndrome)	3
My Random Thoughts	5
Being a Single Mama	5
The Plain Truth	8
Woman of Worth	9
Wow Declaration	9
Women with Issues	11
I Am So Much Better than This!	11
Accept Your Assignment	14
It's Not a Chosen: It's a Given	14
Commitment Issues	16
Demanding Commitment	16
Random Thoughts on Forgiveness	18
The Power to Forgive	18
Put a Ring on It?	20
Be Careful What You Ask For	20
Love in this Club	24
Searching for Mr. Right Now!	24

Spoken Word Moment — 26
    The Raw Deal — 26

No Goods to Spare — 28
    Giving Him the Goods Won't Make Him a Good ANYTHING — 28

Spiritual Ho — 30
    It Takes Two to Tango — 30

Soul Ties — 34
    Why I Can't Tie the Knot — 34

Playing Your Position — 38
    Transition — 38

No More Pain — 41
    Releasing the Past — 41

Time Served — 44

Single Mamas Exposed — 45

Facebook Random Rants — 47

PROVERBS 31 Woman - How Does that Apply to Me? — 50

Single Mothers in the Church — 55

The Issues of Rachel and Leah — 59

Strongholds and Soul Ties — 62

Who's The Man? — 65

Mama Nem Demons — 68

Don't Rush — 72
    To Date or Not to Date — 72

Faith in the Wait — 79

Kill, Steal, and Destroy	83
Walk in Authority	83
Boundaries	85
Status Changes	85
Consecration	89
Mind, Body, and Soul	89
Love Is a Battlefield	93
There's a War Going On!	93
Healing	98
Downtime!	98
Cosmetic Church Consummations	102
"It Just Looks Good"	102
Single and Selective	104
Too Much Thirst and Not Many Standards	104
Be Processed	107
God Is Preparing You	107
Deliverance and Healing	110
Never Alone	110
Recover and Discover	113
Self-Induced Deliverance	113
Dreams and Goals	116
Who Are You?	116
Consecration	119
Close Your Legs, Open Your Ears	119
Fasting and Praying	122
New Beginnings	122

Saved 124
    What Must I Do? 124
About the Author 126

Foreword

Regardless of how you may have become a single mother, be it out of wedlock, divorce, death, or even rape, it is time for you to embrace who you are. Single mothers who are out there and have their children's best interests at heart, to be productive and self-sufficient, all by ensuring their well-being spiritually, emotionally, financially, and physically first before your own, this book is for you. Single mothers who may have made or are making some mistakes along the way, yes, this book is for you also.

There is no book that can teach you how to parent; however, God's Word, the Bible, is a book with a blueprint for all said relationships. Within this book, I have made a conscious effort to provide not only personal accounts of single motherhood, but also with scriptural references for you. Being in ministry, I have learned that there are many who are different from me as it relates to backgrounds; however, many of us have common battlegrounds. As a divorced mother myself, I understand that it's not so easy for others to pick up the pieces and move on, and I understand those mothers who themselves have been hurt and abused too much to fathom the thought of ever being in another relationship. I, also, can understand some of the psyches of those mothers who have only found their identity while being attached to a man.

Clearly, the scope of motherhood and relationships will forever continue to be one of debate when it comes to raising kids and breaking generational footholds, strongholds, and curses. Are you prepared to dig and go deeper into self-evaluation and the realization of how your life as a single mother not only affects you, but also impacts your children, and potentially affects their future relationships? You may not have asked for the title of a single mama; but, regardless of the negative connotations of the term, allow God to show you that the negative does not define you. Single mama is a term that doesn't have to represent the fall or disaster of a relationship with a man; however, it could be the beginning of introducing you to, and beginning, the most important relationship with THE MAN. God is not the author of confusion; trust Him and His plans for your life and your children's lives. I pray this book encourages, strengthens, enlightens, and empowers you.

Acknowledgments

It took me several years to finish writing this book. Not because of poor time management, but simply because of fear. This book has been my special project for some time now and I do believe that God has placed this book within my heart to help other single mothers both inside and outside the church. Being a pastor's and minister's daughter, there are some things that God has allowed life's experiences to challenge, correct, consecrate, and, yes, teach me that in God's permissive will, I am still safe.

Other than my Abba Father Lord and Savior, I thank my parents, siblings, family, and friends. Most importantly, I thank my very own children whom God has blessed me with. You all have made me ultimately a better person. This road has not been easy for my children and me, but we have and shall continue to ride alongside God together.

I also want to acknowledge my leaders and my kingdom family. Wow! I thank God for this new journey with servanthood and doing it with you all.

To my God-sent bestie who is no longer on this Earth, but forever in my heart, I thank you for imparting so much love, wisdom, and understanding, but most importantly, how you taught me the importance of true sisterhood. Forever my Lady!

The Definition of a Real Single Mama

Real Talk

It is with a discerning heart that I put words to paper for my sisters who are dealing with the spirit of guilt. Guilt can consume your very being. You must ask God to deliver you from this hindrance. Look, regardless of how your children came about, rather in or out of wedlock, in love/out of love, GOD still loves you! There is no sin too great for God's everlasting love. The spirit of guilt will keep you in bondage, defensive, and complacent. Release this for the bible says: "Cast all thy cares upon the Lord and he will sustain you" (Psalms 55:22 NIV). I Peter 5:7 NIV states to "cast all your anxiety on him because he cares for you."

God gave you the gift to give life an immeasurable gift. There are no mistakes that He could ever make, so never regret this gift. Regardless of how your child(ren) came about, if that man is no longer a factor, face it, as it's his loss. Your children are not a mistake. God had a divine will and purpose for your life. As the old folk would say, "What doesn't kill you makes you stronger." That's wisdom. Let failed relationships which produced a great product make you a stronger, wiser woman. In life, there is a season for all things, and the season of guilt and shame has got to be released for your season of maturity to manifest. Release seasonal issues so that you may walk into your greatness.

You are a wonderful mother!

I Had to Go Here

GHAMS (Gotta Have A Man Syndrome)

Ok, now I know sometimes you may get a little lonely. The absence of love being reciprocated leads you on a mission of "onto the next one." Fittingly said, a lot of you women have a serious condition of GHAMS (Gotta Have A Man Syndrome). Just any kind of man will do, you have no standards, or perhaps some of you do. Some of you have the prince charming dream - the man who will save you the damsel in distress. The problem is, when does distress digress?

GHAMS seems to be almost the consensus with many women. Most with this syndrome clearly hide this state of being from their families, i.e. home or church. Then, there are some whose names have spread throughout the church like hips and wildfires. Some of you are trying to replace "baby daddies," ex-husbands, boyfriends, or boos by recruiting abroad for your next victim if you will. Yes, VICTIM, because this syndrome is based upon the "get back" factor. You want to get back at your ex for leaving you, so what better way to do it than by replacing him? Now you go through trial and error relationships, which are the basis for the many soul ties you're now struggling with.

"Get back" factor relationships you must understand that you to maybe a get back factor. Gotta Have A Man Syndrome is rooted in bitterness, selfishness, jealousy, and confusion. You are much more than settling for temporary satisfaction. I know that many of you may find humor with my term GHAMS, but we all know one or, in fact, we may be one. Discern with discretion when choosing your mate, ladies… you won't have to look for what God has already pre-ordained.

My Random Thoughts

Being a Single Mama

Being a single mama is not a green light to invite and invade your children's life with different men/women. Single mamas are making it acceptable to spread themselves thin to any man or woman that shows interest. There are repercussions and soul ties that you make your children susceptible to for the sake of your own selfish needs. Stop trying to get back at your baby daddy because this is not a good look. Single mamas, you've had lessons in life on what and where you went wrong, so why continue to make the same mistakes repeatedly? If you met him in the club on Saturday night, he should not be meeting your kids Sunday morning at breakfast.

Red flags:

- If he's not taking care of his own kids. And, please, don't fall for this: "Oh, I don't see my kids because I don't like my ex,"
- If everything he says about his ex is disrespectful.
- If he's living with his mama, his wife, or his baby mama.

Single mamas, you should know by now that you just don't fall in love overnight - so why is Mr. Saturday night residing with you and your kid(s) after only weeks of knowing him?

Things that I ponder on:

- Why do some single mamas "settle" for a man that's worse than the man you had children with?
- Why do some single mamas still lie with the baby daddy who does nothing for his kid(s)?
- Why do some of you single mamas think that putting papers on a man for child support is going to: A. Make him come back to you? B. Make his new woman mad or leave him? C. Make him want to help raise his kid(s)?

My advice to single mamas is that you must do what you gotta do; but, for what emotional price must your child (ren) pay? Raising sons and daughters, is there ever a thought of you being the culprit to the cycle of future unhealthy relationships? Your sons will treat women like how they've seen their mama behave (memo: sorry if you're a ho), then any woman they interact with will more than likely be treated as such. Your daughters will think that it's ok to be treated and regarded as such.

The Plain Truth

It's not about you, anymore plain and simple. Get yourself together before you go "finding" a man to fill those voids in your own life. God blessed you with a kid so that you may do right by them, to unselfishly prepare them to be independent and self-sufficient. Single mamas, don't let this term define you because being a real mama should be your priority! Trial and error with different men is what you want, but not what your kids need. Ok, you're grown and pay your own bills… I get that, but a real man doesn't really want a woman who would put him first before her kid(s). If he is a God-fearing man, he will surely want to seek out the God in you, bottom line. So, stop settling, because you won't have to bother finding what is heaven-sent. He will know where to find you and accept and respect what truly makes you, YOU!

Woman of Worth

Wow Declaration

- ✓ I know who I am and whose I am.
- ✓ Your thoughts of me don't necessarily define me…….
- ✓ I didn't need Maxwell to tell me my worth…
- ✓ God gave it to me from birth…
- ✓ I am a work in progress, but created in God's image, so excuse me, as I am on this road of success and excess…
- ✓ God knows my heart, my thoughts, and my desires…
- ✓ He's been my redeemer, restorer, and provider through the trials of fire…
- ✓ My mishaps had to happen, on my way, my journey, for me to be who I am today…

- ✓ Empowered, delivered, because Jesus Christ paved my way...
- ✓ I know who I am and whose I am...
- ✓ Woman of Worth!

Women with Issues

I Am So Much Better than This!

Many women, not just single mothers, have been victims of various types of abuse. Are you the kind of mother that your child(ren) can feel comfortable with disclosing their innermost feelings to? Do you live the example of a virtuous woman? Or are you a "do as I say, not as I do" mother? Do you subject your child(ren) to your many different relationships because of your selfish heart? Psychology would confirm or suggest that a victim of abuse is highly likely to repeat the same behavior. Most of us attract the same abuse well into our adulthood. Abuse is defined as the systematic pattern of behaviors in a relationship used to gain and or maintain power or control over someone (mincava.umn.edu, 2010).

The Phases of Abuse

Physical: beating, choking, kicking, hitting, etc.

Emotional: verbal attacks on self-esteem/worth, self-image, criticizing, etc.

Psychological: threatening.

Sexual: nonconsensual sexual behavior.

There will surely be some emotional damage as well as psychological distortion for those who believe that you deserve to be abused. As a mother, do you subject your children directly or indirectly to abuse? The Bible story of Tamar (II Sam 13) shows us as women how Amnon "loved" her but not enough to marry her. He, in fact, raped her by way of incest (her step-brother). Tamar was forced to remain quiet, to keep the "dirty" secret. I am sure this led to many feelings such as fear, doubt, and insecurities. Her father failed to protect her and then failed at supporting her. So, what do we as women do when we have had our familial basis disrupted, and we lack protection or support? We grow to accept trivial relationships, which does little to protect (cover) or support us.

Support women often get this misconstrued, with this just being monetary means. However, how many steps must be taken while dancing with the devil? Women with issues who have suppressed abusive relationships will more than likely subject their child(ren) to their feelings of unworthiness. God has made you worthy, you have been vindicated. The word "abuse" becomes past tense when the letter "d" is at the end. It could mean two things for you: either this is a thing of the past or a current condition. This does not mean that you must keep living your life in the past, nor continue to be haunted by things in your past.

Prayer

Lord, I come before You today to ask You to release the spirits of bitterness, unforgiveness, confusion, and abuse. Please forgive those who have blatantly wronged me and those who I have knowingly and unknowingly wronged. I ask for Your strength and in my darkest moments, when my past may surface, please cast down these thoughts. I plead the blood of Jesus on generational curses being removed from my life and those whom I love. In Jesus' mighty name…. Amen

Accept Your Assignment

It's Not a Chosen: It's a Given

I often wonder why so many single mothers lower their standards after bad relationships. I know many who often spiral into those same types of relationships only to be disappointed time after time. They consciously keep making different soul ties and only consider how they feel after the smoke clears. They selfishly put themselves into relationships after relationships while neglecting the very relationships that should be their main priority.

Your relationship with God and your child(ren) should be FIRST!! These are the two relationships that are placed on the back burner while you continue longing to be loved, wanted, and appreciated. Meanwhile, all these feelings can be accommodated right where you are. I am more apt to believe that there is more to life than "chasing" after love. A love undetected leads to the lives of your child(ren) being negatively impacted. They will repeat the very cyclone of habits in which you have subjected them to. The catch-phrase from the movie, *Baby Boy,* "Mama got to have a life too," bothers me to the core. You gave your life in order to give life!!! A single mother is not a chosen title; it is, in fact, a given when circumstances that may be beyond your control involuntarily elects you to carry this title. God has purposed you to be more than a woman, He purposed you to be in His image. Upholding what is right and what is true. God granted women the right to give life which is the greatest gift of all.

Today, say this prayer:

Lord, I thank You for my life and the blessing You have given me to give life. Please make my life and my testimony one that is pleasing in Your sight. Mostly, Lord, make me the woman of God, the mother that YOU will have me to be. Help me to be the mother that You have purposed me to be.

Scriptures

Proverbs 1:8/Ruth 3:11

Commitment Issues

Demanding Commitment

The problem that I've seen is that there is more commitment to non-marital relationships. There are couples who refuse to just walk away, tough things out, while there are those in marriages who seem to lack this very commitment in which marriage was based upon. Marital principles have thus been trivialized to selfish precursors which have led to the rise in divorce rates. From the Christian perspective, is commitment only sacred within a marriage? I struggle with this because some women are more so in love with the fact of being loved, and willing to forego being in a committed relationship. As a single mother, can you demand a committed relationship? In a marriage, I believe this should be a commitment in itself, and unfortunately, you can be committed, and your spouse is unfaithful. So, is commitment contingent upon faithfulness?

Throughout the history of time, women have in a sense been conditioned to accept unfaithfulness. Children being made outside of relationships, (most marriages) and these women remained faithful and committed for the sake of upholding vows. Does this in a sense, as a single mother, make you more acceptable of unfaithfulness? You don't expect a man to be faithful to you because you may not share children with him.

So, have you been conditioned by the four Cs: compromise, convenience, codependence, or circumstance? If you are in a new relationship in which you have committed yourself to, don't let those past experiences of the lack of commitment fester. This man is not him, him of your past. I know it may be hard to fathom that this new man who you may not share any children with can be trusted to remain faithful. Remember that, ultimately, commitment is basically doing the same things all the time. Give yourself the opportunity to forgive and let go; after all, you have moved on.

Random Thoughts on Forgiveness

The Power to Forgive

Do we forgive what we want to forget, thus suppressing? If so, then is forgiveness solely based upon emotion and hence makes it conditional? If God forgives, then why is it so hard for us to do the same? Is it really forgiveness if you can't forget? In the Lord's Prayer, it says: "Forgive us our debts as we forgive our debtors." Analyzing these debts are what we owe which could be symbolic of time, money, etc. Debtors could be symbolic of those who owe us, maybe love, time, patience, or those who are holding us or who we may be held accountable for what is owed in return. Deciding to forgive could ultimately be a hard task for most of us. However, know that God forgives us continuously, consecutively, and unconditionally.

There are many of us who have forgotten that although you may be "saved" now, you haven't always. Truth be told, although you have asked for God's forgiveness of your past transgressions, have you asked those who you may have hurt for their forgiveness. Often, we will see murderers ask for forgiveness from the relatives of their victims. Some may question why, but it is my belief that they ask for forgiveness so that they may forgive themselves. Though in human nature, forgiveness doesn't make wrongs, right per se, but it will make your heart right. You may struggle with people telling you to forgive and forget. Are you to forgive the hurt, pain, and betrayal? Does forgiveness mean that you have exempted those from being accountable for their wrongs?

Be encouraged, my sisters, you should forgive for you to grow. Don't remain stagnant or complacent regarding forgiveness. Sometimes it's necessary to release to increase. Forgive those who said that you would not be a good mother, a good provider, a good woman. After the storms of a bad relationship which has made you have to pick up the pieces and take care of your children all alone, forgiveness is the key. With God, you are never alone and if He grants us brand new mercies everyday forgive those who have wronged you; it will hurt them more to see that you are not bound or caught up in bitterness. Release forgiveness in order to increase in faith.

Put a Ring on It?

Be Careful What You Ask For

According to Beyoncé's acclaimed song, *Put a Ring on It*, quite a catchy song; but, let's be honest, many of you are just not ready for a ring. Really what does a ring signify if you are not in the right state of being? So many are looking for your prince charming and want this man to meet all of these standards when you have absolutely nothing to bring to the table. The analytical side of me questions the song in its entirety.

I personally know several girlfriends who have been given several "rings" throughout the course of their lives, and those rings served only temporary significance. Quite often, they were rings of promises left unfulfilled - like is such a loose term; you could very well like something today, but tomorrow is another story. With all the many marriages around you, but PRIMARILY these "Hollywood" marriages and the prices of these rings are ridiculous. Comparisons of cuts and carats have placed the symbolism of a "ring" as a trivial gift. So with the divorce rates running rampant, I can only conclude that with so many just collecting rings, then why is your focus SOLELY on having that proposal, that wedding gown, that white house with the picket fence? What do you have to bring to the table, because a man may like something about you today; however, when all is said and done, will you let that past hurts surface? Will that prince charming be able to deal with your issues? Prince charming may be overwhelmed with the past and present drama of your "previous" life. You want the ring, but at what cost?

Many meet this prince charming and declare that this man will not discipline your child(ren), guide them with limitations. Meanwhile, your child(ren) remains disobedient, and you need intervention, but you refuse to allow prince charming to be the father figure in this new dream life. So, what is expected of the ring, when you receive it? You are a single mother and have been for a while. First, focus on building a relationship within your home, for when the right man does come along, it will be a union that no man can tear apart. No one said to be lonely, but don't be so driven to get a ring when your life is clearly out of order. No one goes into a marriage seeking to be divorced. Get yourself together, because looks may fade and what may initially make a man fall for you may, in fact, make him fall out with you. You should prayerfully refrain from stirring up more emotional damage, attachment, or detachment issues within you and your child (ren). Be discerning; be careful what you ask for!

This recent Mother's Day, I was so pleased to sit and enjoy a message by my very own mother and she jokingly mocked my niece and my daughter as it relates to this song. My mother challenged the women in the church by changing up the song a little. She said if he likes it, then he will put two rings on it. Now with my mother being "old school," I understand where she was going with this because some of us single mothers can attest to being engaged several times, but never a bride. The engagement ring may be to "shut" you up, but the wedding ring should be to "build" you up!

Women, single mothers - be ever so careful that you don't become in love with thoughts of being loved by a man that you neglect the love from the MAN (GOD). Most often, many mothers are finding themselves settling for the sake of having a man in the house for this fictitious image of what makes up a family's composition, but the man you got in your house doesn't even LOVE your kids. Sadly enough, there is not an ounce of like for your children from "your" man. You are the only one who desires to be unequally yoked because you've accepted a ring and settled for a counterfeit. Be careful what you ask for!!! You must be careful on the mate that you are asking God for; or are have you ever sought God about your potential mate?

Mothers, I cannot stress the importance of seeking God about your mate. Some of you are marrying slicksters and jokesters, or worst - settling by cohabitating with these men who want to run your household off the mere strength of what he's able to do in the bedroom and not his overall work ethic. The work ethics that will help you pay the bills and will help you with that teenage son who is seeking attention or being rebellious. The work ethics of he himself ensuring that he is the head of the household and he is trying in praying with you and your children, going to church not for YOU, but for himself, because he knows that the steps of a good man are ordered by the Lord. He respects that God has called him to fulfill a role within your life and he will not abort, delay, or hinder your relationship's progress. The ring has landed you into a situation where you are constantly in the spiritual warfare for your home. Ain't you tired of crying over the same thing? Ain't you tired of wallowing around in the poor choices you keep making when it comes to who you are choosing? Ain't you tired of someone liking you enough to make you "shut" up by putting the initial engagement ring on your finger, but will not engage himself to your purpose, your calling, your destiny?

Be careful what you ask for!!!

Love in this Club

Searching for Mr. Right Now!

Can you find your ordained relationship in the club? This question, of course, is debatable. Many single women find themselves searching for that "real" love in nightclubs. Women financially invest in their looks and many single mothers find the need to go above and beyond. You can find them auctioning off themselves to the highest bidder from weekend to weekend. Single mamas begin to adopt a "predatory" mentality of looking a certain way will almost guarantee them with some form of commitment. Wrong. Just because you may invest your monies on looking your very best doesn't mean that you will find a man of substance and of good quality.

I have listened to many men who prey on single mothers. They know when a woman says she has kids… bingo, nine times out of ten, these brothers don't want any more kids; so, that's a plus. You drove to the club and invited him back to your house. You seem like you got some independence going on for yourself. You are everything to you, but only a victim of circumstance to these men. Your child(ren) see and most times meet all of these "club loves" you bring home. I know there are a few of you who are saying, "Chile, please! I don't let them meet my kids, and this is probably because Mr. Right doesn't Now stick around long enough to do so. Now we look at the respect factor which has or will become a factor with how your child(ren) view you and ultimately their future relationships. You create the possibility of unstableness, commitment issues, abuse of many forms, along with attachment/detachment issues.

Mr. Right Now may just be serving his purpose with you right now. Analyze your position with him in the long run. Where will Mr. Right Now be in the future tense, single mothers? Stop creating the opportunities for you and your child (ren)to be played out for you being his Ms. Right Now.

Spoken Word Moment

The Raw Deal

- ✓ Wait on him hand and foot; preparing meal after meal, but this single mama is the raw deal…
- ✓ He knows how to reel you back in, manipulates you to sin…
- ✓ You continue to suppress all that he neglects…
- ✓ Withholding the tears and the hurt that's so real… Because you just got the raw deal…
- ✓ Your child(ren) see your hurt and despair…
- ✓ Until numbness takes over…And he is no longer there…

- ✓ When their dad too is no longer there…
- ✓ But, no, this man resides in your mind, your soul, your heart… Those very things you refuse to part…
- ✓ With…for real…
- ✓ Because the raw deal is the truth of the matter, both now and after…
- ✓ Girl, he's not a better man or dad… Just because your soul's been had… He, in fact, is glad you're sad…
- ✓ All signs led to what was real… You are so much more than a…
- ✓ RAW DEAL!!!!

No Goods to Spare

Giving Him the Goods Won't Make Him a Good ANYTHING

I don't know why some of you women continue to lie with men that you're no longer in a relationship with just because you share kids with them. This is the same man that refuses to help support your kids. Well, there are a few of you that think that the man who "pays" his fare (yes, I sure did say it), then it's cool to continue sleeping with your baby daddy(ies). Meanwhile, this is the same man that lives with his "real" woman and his/her kids. You have this make-believe theory that your kids can still see their parents together. Or there's the theory that you can somehow selfishly keep this man in your life; in order words, it ain't got nothing to do with the kids. For those of you who believe that you still got this man, you know the one who has clearly moved on with his life. He is still lying with you because you allow him to. CHY BYE!!! When you wake up from this dream; reality check, you're just his familiar option. So, I have to let you know~ reality check~ giving him your goods will not make him a good daddy.

The Show Must Go On

Bills, bills, bills…

Kids, kids, kids…

The show must go on…

Even when there is no "real" man at home…

Pick up the pieces and find your way because the show must go on…

Through every trial or struggle day by day…

Seek to better yourself… Even when there is no one else…

In all things, get understanding….

When things seem so overwhelming and demanding…

Focus on the things that you are obligated to… Because…

The show must go on with or without you…

Dedication to my sisters to encourage you to keep on pushing*

Spiritual Ho

It Takes Two to Tango

Yeah, you know her!! Sister so and so ain't nothing but a spiritual ho. Very forward, but my apologies, it's so true. There are so many women who frequent the clubs as much as they frequent the church. You know the ones who work their way wickedly through the church smiling and grinning at every man that makes eye contact. These women profess their love for God and secretly harbor in their heart's lust. Women who will do anything for a man, especially a church-going man. In these days and times, a woman who is saved is equally attracted to those within and outside the church. I classify the spiritual hoes into four categories:

First up ~ the "hope the pastor notices me" women.

Secondly~ "I hope this church got some fine men" women.

Thirdly, we have the women~ "I'm going after any man that holds a position in the church." Lastly are the "girl, he 'go' to church" women.

In the Bible, in the story of Bathsheba, her significance was that she did not do anything out of the ordinary, initially. David clearly fell to his weakness. Isn't it just amazing how the enemy knows how to play on our very weaknesses? As a single mother who is trying to live her life right before the Lord, there will be many temptations you may be confronted with. These may serve as true tests of your faith and faithfulness. Some of you have had past struggles and lifestyles in which in your saved life try to surface again.

Bathsheba, although we can find many things wrong with her in this story, proves that it takes two to tango. How many tangos must you tie yourself to before you realize that just because it feels good to you, doesn't mean that it's right for you? Do you continue to compromise your life living for God for your fleshly desires? The walk of purity and salvation may, in fact, be a lonely road to tread upon. However, know that you have been built and equipped for such a time as this. Do you compromise or distort your children's perception or image of you or God for selfish soul ties? Truth be told, you can't have an overly trusting heart when inviting those into your dwelling place. Your body is a temple; the bible teaches us to present our bodies as a living sacrifice. Romans 12:1 (NIV): "Therefore, I urge you, brothers (sisters), in view of God's mercy, to offer your bodies as living sacrifices, holy and pleasing to God - this is your spiritual; an act of worship." In the book of Peter Chapter 2:11 (NIV): "Dear friends, I urge you as aliens and strangers in the world, to abstain from sinful desires which war against your soul."

Now, this is powerful "to abstain from sinful desires which war against your soul." Too many women focus on what makes us "fleshly" happy this includes physical happiness, instead of emotionally, mentally, and spiritually complete. Sinful desires war against the soul because desires are, in fact, flesh-driven, which are compromised by emotional desires. Desires of the flesh disagree with the Spirit and the will of God. When we desire to have and do all the things that are in opposition to God's will, we always end up with temporary solutions. When we understand that dating does not mean submitting or being held captive to our fleshly nature, we understand the concept of dating ourselves first.

The flesh is indeed weak, this is so true, but with every carnal encounter, we introduce ourselves to different circumstances. You can be a saved single mother who is dating without being a ho. Remember you are responsible for setting the boundaries. I am just going to be very matter-of-factly if you don't love everybody you have chosen to be intimate with. Some of you have hidden secrets and pains in which you need to seek deliverance. As a mother, we have to ensure that we break this generational curse so that our very own children don't continue the cycle of "fleshly" happiness. Firstly, every man that you entertain a conversation with doesn't even deserve that much; but nevertheless, every man that you choose to allow say those sweet-filled lies into your ear gates is not assigned to you!

Soul Ties

Why I Can't Tie the Knot

Women, by nature, are emotional beings, and many find it hard to differentiate the differences between giving love and being loved. I am often reminded of the powerful sermon preached by Dr. Juanita Bynum, "No More Sheets." Dr. Bynum's discussed the awesome correlation of being entangled in sheets with the many physical, emotional, mental, and spiritual relationships in which she had experienced. This message continues to be a powerful message on women struggling with virtuous relationships.

As women, we must understand that throughout our lives, we exchange our energy, which is then connected with those of which we share interactions. Most of those interactions, of course, have been or are physical. These become soul ties that become un-seemingly impossible to break. Soul ties are in fact an act of bondage or manipulation at its finest. Women find themselves being prone to manipulation. The manipulation happens in all facets, such as when a man keeps controlling you like a puppet through the process of what I call the "means of things." Means of things include money, cars, jewelry, and trips, but mostly sex. So why do we allow ourselves to firstly fall victim to unhealthy soul ties? We mistake the physical aspects of relationships for self-sought love. We seek to gain that so-called man of our dreams, regardless of how he may treat us.

Are soul ties keeping you in bondage today? Holding on to those past relationships may be the reason why you can't and won't tie the knot! Some of the men you have been choosing to have are there because you pursued them. As uninvited guests, your children look at these characters that you are allowing into their lives while placing such high expectations upon them and yet Tyrone or Pookie can do the minimal. You think a man loves you because if he is not employed, he pushes a vacuum around the house, maybe takes the trash out, or cooks dinner from food that you purchased.

Ladies, mothers, it is time to become real with you. Your title ~ your purpose in this man's life is simply CONVENIENCE. Ms. Convenience! Meanwhile, your new boo, love, new husband (in some instances), your title of convenience, has made it an inconvenience to everything and everyone else in your life. Your relationships with everyone else is suffering and being negated, and disregarded. Everything will suffer a loss and lose its importance in your life when you are unequally yoked.

Self-assessment:

You're accustomed to living a certain way: your children have structure; there is a household routine as it relates to homework, housework, etc. When you get connected to someone who does not want to build with you and your children, please do a self-assessment of where you are right now at this moment right now. Sometimes you have been preying on a man that another woman has been praying for to get right and because you were willing to accept him as he is, he's free to do himself long as he is doing you!!! Entangled in sheets and in the matters of the heart!!! It is time to break free.

Prayer:

Lord God, I pray and declare and decree that the sister reading this is no longer bound by temporary fleshly pleasures. Lord God, I pray that she is strengthened to stop accepting and settling for less than when YOU oh most holy God have better and more than she could ever imagine waiting for her. Let her trust your timing; give her faith over feelings right now, Father God. Give her comfort and the peace of knowing that there is a man that You will place on her path so there is no need to pursue.

Sister, I beckon you to stop being free in the mighty name of Jesus. There is no need to pursue a man, as God has him in his timing and he will find you. You can't find him because he is supposed to find you. Let go, let God.

Playing Your Position

Transition

I am an avid lover of the game of basketball. Just like any other sports, there are players who play certain positions on a team. What is so significant about the different positions? Some seem to think that it is, in fact, the player, who is more important than the position. My perception of this is: What will the player do in his/her given position? What will a player do when his/her position is threatened or compromised? When a situation occurs that would change your position, do you give up? The transition from the past to future may be a hard task. Many of us are still dealing with bad relationships which caused us to become bitter. But I speak transition to the next level in your life. Former relationships have left many with children to raise alone.

It's ok my sisters; God hears your prayers. You must play with the cards you've been dealt and play your position.

Transition doesn't feel good all the time, nor does it always make sense. The word "transition" itself means to change from one position, stage, subject, or movement. What's significant is that we remain focused when transitioning from another position to another. A lot of single mothers or women in general may have their reservations about change. Change, unfortunately, is one of life's guarantees; yes, it is bound to happen, and it will happen. As we transition into motherhood at each various stages or phases in our children's lives, it becomes harder to let go. Our eyes cannot lie, what we do see is truly the development of our daughters or sons.

Single mothers often find themselves adapting to their environment involuntarily of those who feel as if they have forfeited their own lives and look upon their children's age progression as a green light to their very own freedoms. Transition within a single mother's home is always a constant with many of them not maintaining a sense of stability financially, spiritually, emotionally, and quite often mentally. A single mother struggles with trying to play both parental roles within one household. Quite often, it's a gamble to say the least. Many single mothers swear off the fathers out while playing to part and acting on queue. Single mothers become great actresses, smiling on the outside while excessively hurting on the inside. Transition seems to be the norm within the single mother's household while she adapts to the various tests and the hard blows of life.

We must be willing to embrace change which will duly change your position on a lot of levels. Transition sets forth positional change, and as a single mother, you must know your position throughout transitional changes. Transition yourself voluntarily, by the changing and the renewing of your mind. It is very often that many single mothers find themselves lonely while either longing for past relationships or seeking numerous new relationships. Transitioning themselves into those who live with regrets of those who have transformed into the mindset of "get them before they get you" syndrome. Along the phases of transformation, bitterness, brokenness, sadness, often imbrues their very existence.

Transition, change, and transform your mindset today! You cannot productively or proactively rear your children for successful interactions with the opposite sex. Will the ideologies of your past and/or present relationships consist of the many different faces of multiple changes? Consistency will be key in their lives, and ultimately your life.

No More Pain

Releasing the Past

R&B artist Mary J. Blige penned and belted one of my favorite songs to date, *No More Pain*. Those three words were and still are so significant because it places an expiration date on pain. No more, no mas; pain cannot reside in you anymore. As single mothers, there is often pain associated with failed relationships. All the questions of why, how, what surfaces to our core and leaves many with trust issues. Oftentimes, single mothers regress these feelings and leave themselves to wear their hearts on their sleeves. Abandonment issues tackled by trust issues lead to fear of the unknown. Weighing factors of your own self-image, you question why he left you (for her)? *How could he do me like this? What did I do to deserve this?*

Sisters, it is important to know that these questions embody pain. Too many single mothers are willing to settle for the so-called Mr. Right when he is completely and totally all wrong. I must thank one of my Pastors with saying we pray for husbands knowing full well whom we are currently entertaining our time, energy, and efforts on are not capable of reciprocating what we're voluntarily giving. In other words, we opt for praying for husbands that are not even capable of holding a friend title. He is all wrong for you!!! We should be praying that, "God, Thy Will Be Done" when seeking a mate.

Many people struggle with juggling acts, holding auditions and casting calls, accepting resumes of unworthy applicants for the position of husband. Many single mothers become so fearful of being alone that they accept "just any old man will do" mindset. This man does nothing to edify you spiritually, emotionally, mentally, nor financially. Some of us opt for being surrogate mothers to under-mothered men. Hurt after hurt; time after time, meanwhile, anger builds and you're soon mentally incapacitated. What should have brought about a level of growth and maturity was in fact an onset of clear immaturity.

Let's face it, some of us of Delilah often transform into many of the men we choose to entertain. You were doing just fine before you gave into this Delilah spirit on Tony, Mark, or Bobby. Mothers, do not make yourself an easy target for predators, who seek to prey on you and not pray for you; or with you. Pain does not have to beget more pain. You must make a decision today that, as Mary put it, "I am never gonna hurt again; No More Pain."

Time Served

It would be easy to walk away from you, but love done got a hold on me…

It would be easy to pretend like you didn't matter to me, but love done got a hold on me…

It would be easy to say that I don't love or care about you, but love done got a hold on me…

It would be easy to reminisce on all the wrongs you've done, but love done got a hold on me…

It would be hard to forget your smile, but love has released me…

It would be hard to leave you in my past, but love has released me…

It would be hard to allow you back here in my heart because love once had a hold on me but now the same love has released me and my time has been served!

Time Served

Single Mamas Exposed

The single mother who is consumed with work and making up for what the absent father doesn't provide. Be it overextending herself with time, and money to compensate for their child's loss of emotional, mental, physical, spiritual needs. This maybe you! Then we have the single mother who spends most of her time in wait mode. This mother is waiting on a check (be it government or payroll, let me say that), waiting on a faulty child support system to deem your request for these monies as legitimate, which now has you waiting on a paternity test. The waiting game continues for the single mother who waits for her child's father's release date. Yes, release date from prison so she waits patiently until his return or decides to enjoy this waiting period by dating other people. Then we have the waiting single mother who believes that she should wait for any man to come along and fill the shoes or the role of boyfriend or boo (but not husband) just to help her out on some of the bills. This type of single mother spends her time just waiting on some source or entity to relieve some of the pressures of daily life duties and the pressures of raising kids alone. Is this you? The single mama who doesn't have time for her kids for the reasons of work, school, other people, habits, or anything that takes precedence over your kids… is this you?

It is important for single mothers to recognize that you carry the power to break any generational curses; you have the power to IMPART, IDENTIFY, and INTERCEDE on behalf of your children. Stop telling your kids they are going to be just like such and such because you are harboring feelings of guilt, resentment, and hatred towards the absent parent, your parents, or the other DNA's parents. The curse may not have begun with you, but purpose today that it will end with you. God has a plan for you and your children and contrary to popular opinion you are worth more alive than dead. It is God's will that you shall live as well as prosper.

The absent parent will have their own cross to bear should it warrant that; your children do not need you "mama" talking bad about their missing, inactive, father. You do more harm than good while trying to appear more than or better than him. Learn to be at peace with the choices and the decisions you have made.

True, nobody asks to be a single parent, but if that is what life has rendered, then have faith in God that He shall supply all your needs. The word says that in Psalm 37:25 NLT: "Yet I have never seen the godly abandoned or their children begging for bread." Trust in God and not in a man, not in a check, not in a job, to help you take care of your children. Jesus is your help, even though you may not feel you can do anything without the help of a man, a check, or a job. But put your trust in God Almighty, JEHOVAH JIREH.

Facebook Random Rants

Don't expect for your kids to respect you being double-minded and living a double life. This day and time is not a time of "do as I say, not what I do" if what you're doing is contradictory to what you're saying. Practice what you preach/speak. Stop expecting expectations of your children that you are respectively failing in. I'm sorry, but all this clubbing and partying at some of y'all ages are just ...as old as you are. If you haven't experienced "fun" by now in your life, then get over it! These kids are seeking love and attention that they can't even get at home. Unfortunately, from the streets, it comes with a heavy price.

Ladies, it's getting ridiculous... I don't care about learning these kids' latest dance and fashion trends. You should recognize that all this stuff is just history repeating itself. Stop going from bar to bar~ listening to this "RAH RAH" music, meanwhile, your kids don't get you any top honors. Quite frankly, it's sad that you're older but stuck in a childlike mentality. The title of mama isn't a given because you gave birth! Acting like one does. Instead of trying to mother these un-mothered men, be a mother to the kids God has blessed you with. Some of you have more patience for the apathetic men you're choosing and zero patience, time, and tolerance for your own seed. We can say these kids are different, these kids are this and that all we want, but when they see you living what you say and doing what you say, then maybe we will see a real change. What example are you giving/showing yours? Wake up!!

In one split second, your life can change for the better or for the worse. Just learned earlier today that one of my oldest sons' AAU Basketball teammate's life has drastically changed for the worse. I know, single mothers, it may be challenging raising kids alone with no or little support from the absent parent. Don't stop being a parent for the price of being a "friend." You should NEVER be too busy to be a parent. God should always be first in your life and your children. I still check phones. Why? Because I pay the bills! I still demand respect of me and elders. Know your children's friends and know their whereabouts. Plead the blood of Jesus over them. Will they make mistakes? Yes. But some can be avoided if you take your responsibility more serious and PARENT!

While you're making excuses on why you can't do this or that, these streets are calling their name. Stop rushing your boys out into these streets they're not yet prepared for. God is calling you to accountability. Ain't no man/ woman, job, career etc. worth you giving your children to the streets to raise. My heart is heavy right now... Stop settling for these no-good men and expect your boys to be great men. They just celebrated winning a championship not even 2 weeks ago. God has equipped you for the task of being a mother; He has blessed you with the gift of being a mother. I thank all the dads who actively support their children, not by monetary means but those who are present! Truth is, some of you mothers may be present, but you have no presence... Lord, these youth need your help. Women...single mothers, no excuses. Surely, it hasn't been an easy road for me, but by the grace of God, He is your help. #praying

PROVERBS 31 Woman - How Does that Apply to Me?

The 31st Proverb is often a passage of scripture which many have modeled many women conferences, workshops, a blueprint or in fact the formula for the example of a godly woman, a godly wife, a godly mother, and a godly servant. It is an opinion as well that this chapter of Proverbs remains to be so relevant and profound. I believe that the name of the woman referenced within this chapter was omitted, it was made anonymous, for a reason. Often, we get so caught up with names and titles, but when we look at this woman she had no name. Her character spoke louder than her words. Her actions complemented her character. As a single mother, it is important that your actions complement your character. You can't be a great mother and spiritually corrupt or lack a personal relationship with God. Every mother, regardless of socioeconomic status, should seek an openly visible relationship with God.

As a single mother, you find yourselves totally dependent on yourself because there are not as many people who can help for the many times that you may need it. Responsibilities right and left, bill after bill, need after need. I want you to know to cast your cares upon the Lord. He is a very present help in your time of need. No, it is not going to be easy, but a good mother is a worshipper, she praises the Lord, and she is a woman whose character carries the spirit of faith, the spirit of a fighter. She understands the importance of breaking the yokes of poverty, the importance of breaking the yoke of lack, the importance of breaking the yokes of dysfunction, the yokes of unforgiveness, and as a result of her being spiritually in tune to this, she makes it imperative that she exercises the actions necessary to ensure that her children, although may have been subjected to these elements or spirits, do not succumb to them.

Single mothers, I know many of you when attending these many conferences wonder how you identify with the Proverbs 31 woman because the focal point that has always been talked about is that she was married; she had a husband. Some of you single mothers are currently in this classification due to divorce, and separation and you were the Proverbs 31 woman within this relationship and now because of the demise of this relationship, many of you have grown bitter instead of better seeking Rita instead of Robert. Understand that this will introduce your children to another onslaught of more emotional soul ties, and quite possibly more confusion. Since the past attempt of being a Proverbs 31 woman, you have gone from being committed to one to now being uncommitted to many. You can be a Proverbs 31 woman again in another relationship with the God-ordained man that God has set apart for you; and only for you. A man that findeth a wife findeth a good thing; the man, your potential spouse, is then blessed because you are the carrier of the blessing for his life. So, there is no need to fret over your current status. If you're not married now, that does not mean that the Proverbs 31 woman's status of being married was the only thing to her. These qualities which made up her character had to already pre-exist within; it may have been taught or just God-given and inspired by God.

It is important that you realize that she wasn't a great woman because of what she had; she was a good woman because of what she did; she was a good woman just because that is who she was. Her character and her abilities to act upon and rise to the occasion were a part of her. What was instilled within quite naturally became a part of her character. What are you instilling within your child or your children? What values, morals, and character traits will you be responsible for, which will have an influential and inspirational impact within their lives? It is imperative that regardless of if you were a Proverbs 31 woman or a Gomer, God can change anyone. All we need to do is take the first step and repent- ask for forgiveness of our shortcomings.

These descriptions could also be found when David's parents were seeking a mate, a help mate, for their son. His mother gave him the characteristics of what a good woman is. While pondering on this part of the book and the revelation that I received from the Holy Spirit in regard to the Proverbs 31 woman, I believe that her description is that of herself. What mother would not want her son to have a wife that has her qualities? What is important about this, says the Holy Spirit, is that you as a mother do not become so critical and judgmental of your sons or daughters' potential mates. What is crucial in their relationships is that you refrain from imposing your very own beliefs as to what a good mate is especially if it has been hard for you to maintain one healthy relationship. As a mother, it is important that you ensure that your son is capable of being a productive man should he be without a spouse until a certain time in his life. Your son should be prepared to take care of himself and be prepared to take care of a family. These values must be instilled and must be set as an expectation.

Mothers, your daughters should never have to experience an identity crisis as to what is a good woman, a good wife, a good mother, overall good and well-equipped woman. She should know how to care for a home and know how to care for a husband. The fact of the matter that you decided not to remarry or marry altogether should never be imposed upon your daughter's future in experiencing this. It is important that your daughter understands that a Proverbs 31 woman was many things, but out of all the characteristics that she exuded, she was a stable woman mentally and emotionally. Many of you mothers need to reevaluate your mental and emotional state while raising your kids alone. Are you emotionally and mentally stable enough to instill the values and morals of what a good man and/or woman is? Is your mental and emotional condition after the breakup or after the divorce healthy? This is vital to their development of relationships because your poor emotional and mental state is subject to being evaluated under the small microscope of their eye and questioned within the large mirror of minds.

Do you blame your children for the failed relationship? Some of your mothers need to repent from the spirit of anger. Your child or children is not the reason that relationship failed. The relationship failed because two adults were not on the same accord or just wasn't meant to be. I am a realist when it comes to matters of the heart. That failed relationship may have served as the closed door because it wasn't healthy; it was abusive, it lacked God. Some people stay in these types of relationships thinking that they will remain for the sake of the children, and in the end, the children have a false sense of what a real relationship is. They grow up thinking that they must put up with being abused, misused, cheated on, and lied to. They grow up thinking that any dysfunction that it is within the range of human normalcy is acceptable. They too decide to repeat the cycle of choosing poor mates, making bad decisions, compromising who God has created them to be to settle for what a man or woman say they are. This continues the generational curse of poor relationships and the onslaught of denial and poor mental stability. If the relationship is ordained from God, I am just a firm believer that whatever is not right has to become right. Stop dating men that you would not want your daughters to marry or your sons to become.

Single Mothers in the Church

*I*n these days and times, I have heard that the "black" church keeps many women single. There are a few articles readily assessable that support the idea that the black church keeps many single women single. Everyone is entitled to their opinion; however, I do not believe that it is the church per se; I believe that there is certainly a new level of standards and requirements that many single women who are single mothers begin to adopt after many years of trying to do things alone and the fact that they have relied heavily and solely within the constraints of a paycheck and the grace of God to get them through. Then we have the single mother who sees the church as the new meet and greet; their local hook-up spot to connect the dots with any man that comes into the church.

Sadly enough, church begins to be a breeding ground for many desperate women who are looking for love, money, companionship, in men that God has not anointed them to be yoked to. Guest speakers become open prey of many single women and single mothers who are attracted to physical appearances or just the fact of the gender; the overall fact of a man who doesn't know them or what issues or baggage they come with. As a daughter of a pastor myself, I have witnessed from a very young age how women look for a ring; when most people, men or women, do not even wear wedding bands thinking that this is an invitation to pursue this man of God. Sadly enough, a lot of women do not care. If they do see a ring, they see the title, the anointing, the position, a MAN…. Single women and mothers, please note that there are some things that God has not anointed you to do meaning that just because you're single doesn't mean that a man is not supposed to have his very own standards. An anointed man of God may be seeking the same in his potential mate or you may need to watch out for the man of God who only believes that the man is anointed, and he wants a woman who can merely respect his calling and neglect her very own.

Slow-down bad relationships occur outside the church as well as inside the church. Make sure you're anointed enough to carry the oil you're chasing. I am reminded of the story of Leah and Rachel; in the Bible, in the 29th chapter of Genesis, we are introduced to these sisters, and although, sisters, there were some things that differed with these sisters. Both daughters of Rachel, the "fine" sister who appeared to have it all together was whom Jacob fell in love with, just from her beauty, her body, as the Word stated that she was beautiful in "form and face." The contrast between the sisters begins when the word references that Rachel's eyes were bright and Leah's eyes were said to be dark. A fact that stands out to me is the fact that Jacob fled Beersheba because his life was in danger. Through the long and tiresome journey of going to the land of his mother, there is where he first laid eyes upon Rachel. The bible clearly makes note that Rachel was the beautiful sister and Leah was the less attractive sister. Shortly, I will go into the underlying message to the "modern day" sisters.

In this biblical story, one can derive many preachments and/or studies from this, but I am going to focus on the fact of women destroying other women when there is a man involved. Rachel's rivalry with her very own sister, Leah, poisoned her relationship not only with her sister, but also with Jacob. Leah was the sister whom God made very fruitful while Rachel was barren.

As I look deeper into the story of the sisters, it is a reminder of the fact that we as women spend so much time and effort in our appearances. Some women go through extreme measures to appease the opposite sex, but Rachel and Leah shed some light on some once personal convictions and proclivities. People can truly "judge a book by its cover" incorrectly. Rachel's beauty did not bring her contentment, as she had a very jealous heart. Although Jacob loved her deeply, Rachel was still unhappy. Leah, on the other hand, sheds some light on the fact that people can look at the outer appearance of a person, not necessarily what may quicken an immediate response or attraction, but maybe whom God has assigned to help you focus on Him.

I would recommend anyone to read this story of the two sisters and the twists and turns within the story, and how this story ministers about the depths, the things people put themselves through for love, and even the things God allows within the growing pains of loving too hard, or basically not loving enough. Please take the time to feel free to take some notes after reading this. What are some things that God has revealed to you about yourself? Have you placed your worth in the hands of another to validate who you are? Do you feel like you are not worthy of being loved? Do you feel like your value is worth the minimal efforts because you may not look like someone else; yes, even your birth sister, work sister, church sister, neighborhood sister? Do you think that because you may not appear to have any outer flaws, you are not privy to your heart being broken? Or do you think because you appear to be beautiful and have it all together, people misjudge you wrong? Are you the beautiful one who really has the lowest self-esteem issues, hates your very image, jealous, and unloving? Are you the sister who enjoys helping others, no matter how bad they may make you feel, because your only desire is in pleasing others and wanting to be accepted?

Please use the next couple of pages to journal about how you really feel about yourself. What are some of the characteristics that you may share with both Rachel and Leah? Pray about the poor self-image you have of yourself. Begin to focus on the areas in which you can change and seek deliverance about the strongholds that doesn't make it easy for you to do it alone. Only the love of God will be the one stable force in all of our existence.

The Issues of Rachel and Leah

*L*ord, I may not be America's Next Top Model, but, in my opinion, I think I look good enough. I may not be a size 2 or 6, but I think my clothes fit pretty good on me. No, I am lying, I hate my body, because nobody ever appreciated it until they wanted it or needed it. I hate the way I look in the mirror because it's a reflection of the abuse, the misuse, the hits, the blows, the cellulite; the rolls, wait a minute, I really don't see all that. Could it be that I have been made to feel like that? What do others see when they see me? Do they see beauty? Or do they see ugly? No, I am not America's Next Top Model, but I think I can give someone a run for their money or either take their money; my looks alone can make anyone love me.

Well, if that's the case then why am I all alone? Why didn't he answer his phone? Wait a minute, could I be so caught up in myself that he doesn't know how else to show me that he loves me? He loves me like Lydel in E flat, thanks to Jill. Can I use my looks to pay a bill? Or two? Hold up because I can't be the one just doing anything for a dollar. When I look in the mirror, I don't see myself as pretty, so why even bother. Men have used my quirks, what seems to be abnormalities to me for the sake of getting over on me. I heard I am ugly I should be glad I have somebody. Just met a beautiful sister who says she feels alone but has everybody and everything it seems. The crazy part about it, we both have poor self-esteem.

Rachel and Leah, I know how you feel!

Journal

Self-Image and Self-Identity

Strongholds and Soul Ties

A stronghold is merely a thinking pattern which is based upon deceptions and lies. As we know, the devil, our enemy and adversary, uses deception to launch an all-out attack against us because it is the beginning of creating strongholds. Strongholds are the results of deceit, the stumbling block that will block us or keep us from having God's very best for us. Seeing God incorrectly and seeing yourself incorrectly are the foundations of what keeps many in bondage and leads many to unconfessed sins, as well as unaddressed sins. Strongholds have many of you caught in what seems to be an unbreakable bond to soul ties. I have learned throughout my lifetime that strongholds, as well as soul ties, are closely related. When wanting to break free of a soul tie, it is important to understand that a stronghold is a mindset that's in complete opposition to God's written word. We allow strongholds in our lives by feelings and by our thoughts. So, it is important that when wanting and desiring to be free of strongholds and unhealthy soul ties, that deliverance from even yourself is needed.

Changing your thought pattern, I know is better said than done, but freedom from the stronghold begins here. What I find, as being led by the Holy Spirit, is that there are many older women who have been living in their very own prisons all their lives. These women have allowed strongholds and unhealthy soul ties to make them bitter. Now, the Bible instructs the older women to "train the younger women"; however, how can these women train the younger women to love and intercede for their husbands when most of them settled for marrying the wrong spouse, took someone else's spouse, or were the spouses who were left for someone else and have lived with this hurt and disappointment for the majority of their lives. It kind of makes me wonder how many of our existing church mothers who are regarded as mean and callous could be because they are bound and have become bitter as a result of soul ties. The issue becomes problematic because we see an ongoing generational stronghold which swallows up the trust of fellow laypersons within the church and within every acquaintance, associate, or relationship generally acquired in life.

So how does one begin to acknowledge a stronghold and identify the soul ties which have them bound? If you find yourself still talking about what somebody (the soul tie) made you do and what they did, and it makes you bitter, emotional to some degree, sad, or even happy, quite possibly you are still bound. Especially if you are in another relationship and the new spouse is constantly being compared to the ex. DING DING DING, this is a stronghold as well as a soul tie. Will you be honest enough with yourself to get free? Now onto those of you mothers, how do strongholds and soul ties tie into this topic? If you have children with a previous mate and have remarried or have a new relationship with someone else and you have had children with the new mate, and are treating the previous child indifferent because you are not with his or her father, then this is a problem. A big problem! If the child with the new mate receives preferential treatment versus the previous child, then again, the same thing, this is a problem. Children should never suffer any emotional, spiritual, verbal, or physical distress due to the fact of you being in bondage. This makes the chances of them repeating the very exact same behaviors, choices, and/or decisions very high. Mothers, our roles within our children's lives is a ministry within itself. Unfortunately, many do not get to understand or embrace that until time has slipped away from you.

Who's The Man?

I've heard of many sayings, quotes, and clichés over the span of my life~ in my wilderness experience, in Lo Debar, or even within the times of going untested. The anointing attracts attacks! With that said you can believe the saying, "If you're anointed, prepare to be disappointed." I've heard many of these statements; quite frankly, it is my belief that this is the reason many run the opposite way. The times of testing and trying can be extreme, and the facts of the pain and the evidence of what appears to be a daily debacle of your life can rip at the very core of your being. Many single mothers in this testing phase, this phase of loneliness, this phase of uncertainty, this phase of confusion, think the answer is wrapped up in an earthly man.

Truth of the matter is that this is the time that God has personally considered you to focus on Him. Could you hear Him then when you were comfortable in an unauthorized relationship? Could you hear Him when there were no pressures, and all your bills were paid; you and your children were in good health. Could you hear God when your credit scores, when your salary afforded you many material pleasures in life that you really felt as though you didn't need anybody? Did you acknowledge Abba Father God during these times? Did you fathom the thought that He was your provider? Did you give credit to God or did you show praises to earthly men? Was it your man, be it a boo or a now estranged spouse, the job man, the rent man, the postman? What man have you placed before the Lord? What men have you allowed to have God's glory?

The bible specifically notes and records that God is a jealous God. I understand that many will advise women that their spouse is the head over her, but we are living in a day and time where many of you women got married young, out of obligation to man and not out of reverence for God. You were married to please a man and not the MAN. Hence causing an unequally yoked marriage. I know there will be a backlash from this; however, as a daughter of a pastor and a minister, trust me, there is not too much that I haven't heard regarding this. I will go into this in detail in another chapter, but for now, the focus point is on whom have you placed above God. What men have you made idols out of? The book of Exodus primarily dealt with a lot of idol worshipping. The children of Israel, out of frustration and the uncertainty in if God was going to come through for them. It becomes easy for one to fall into "idolizing" or "idol worship" because whom we placed in this role we can see, feel, and touch. It's the corruption of our hearts from life's voids that presents opportunities to fall into some form of idolatry. Who you place in these dark places of voids can only be a CARNAL sense of worship!

God is commanding that you no longer offer Him carnal worship; He is commanding you to do away with contaminated worship. God has been trying to get your attention during the testing times while He's patiently watching you make idols out of men, money, etc. He's been asking you, "Who's The Man?" However, you couldn't hear Him over the noise, the pleasurable and convenient distractions. Now that He has your undivided attention, they that worship Him must worship Him in spirit and in truth!! (John 4:24).

Mama Nem Demons

Many times, we try to attempt to get ahead of God when it comes to things in our lives, and what happens? Something good may come out of it, but it won't last. Something good may come out of it, but it's not for your overall good. I know many jump head first on many things because we as humans do not want to take the time to discern the times and be still long enough or quiet the madness of our daily lives to hear God's voice. Mothers, it is important in times when it appears you cannot hear from God; it is very important that you surround yourself around individuals who can hear from God. During the times when you can't trace God, surround yourself with those who can prophetically see and hear what thus sayeth the Lord for your life. However, it is important that you're not familiar with these people.

Many of you have sought counseling and/or opinions from those who already know everything about you or even what people in your bloodline are known for. For example, "Oh well, her mama has never been in a long-term relationship; she has four baby daddies and two ex-husbands." You catch my drift. Women, it is important that you know your identity and stop attaching and associating your identity to generational curses and bondages. We have an epidemic of "CAN'T WAIT." How many times must you continue to make the same repeated mistakes, if mama nem gave you example after example on when not waiting on God goes wrong? When you can't deny your own fleshly desires, this will surely bring about poor choices, and, yes, demonic soul ties.

I know it's very hard for you to even fathom the very thought that every woman you are related to has been flirty, or as I grew up hearing, *fast*. Yes, even your grandmother may have some explaining to do when it comes to questions about the father of one of her very own children. Some of our elders seem to have forgotten that they have not always been saved; they haven't always been holy or sanctified. Quite frankly, if they had done their jobs effectively, our parents would not have been shunned in the church for having babies out of wedlock and forced into many unhealthy and abusive marriages, and our generation and coming ones are left to fight with mama nem's demons. If mama nem would have taken the time to see about deliverance from their very own demons and their predecessors, it could have very well prevented many of the struggles that we have experienced or are currently experiencing now.

It could be that you were molested as a young girl by an uncle, grandfather, brother, sister, your dad, your mother or grand mother's boyfriend/girlfriend, or just a family member. Those demons need to be addressed, acknowledged, so that you can get delivered and healed. The spirit of perversion is the parent demon that gives birth to several other demonic possessive spirits. If you are not in a church that believes in deliverance, then I would suggest you do your research on getting delivered and being set free from those suppressed demons and hidden family secrets that have kept many of your family members, before you came along, in bondage. Will the generational curses stop at you? Will mama nem's demons be demised by you? I would recommend you find an apostolic deliverance ministry in which both men and women of God operate in the prophetic as well as deliverance ministry. You may make all the difference in your family's lifeline. Many of your family members will take these demons and hidden secrets to their graves. Bondage will become a thing of acceptance instead of relevance. It is time to break the chains of bondage to lose the chains of destructive and disastrous choices that only leads to more self-inflicted bondages and soul ties. It's time to let mama nem's demons die.

Sometimes God must place you in solitary confinement for you to look at yourself. Looking in the mirror shouldn't just be to examine what may be our physical imperfections and flaws, but rather looking deeper inside to what is internally scarred within us. There are some scars that from the physical eyes are hidden deep and we try with much human effort to keep these facts that are ugly about us from surfacing. Many women have tried to mask hidden scars with makeup, material things, and, yes, even men. Some women have truly lost their sense of self and value by associating how they ultimately feel about themselves with the intention of "getting" a man. We can find many women with this same ideology within any environment, even within the confines of our local worship places.

God wants you to see yourself as He sees you!! You are fearfully and wonderfully made. We too were created in His image as outlined in the "beginning," GENESIS 1:27. God felt that Adam needed and was worthy of a helpmate and along came Eve in Chapter 2. God orchestrated a blessing while Adam was asleep. God performed the first surgery on Adam to bring his blessing, his God-ordained blessing, to pass. God presented Eve to Adam as a gift; you are the added blessing to your assigned Adam's life. If it's God-sent, you won't have to force it, nor lose or compromise all of who you are to keep it!

God has a special man in mind that is anointed and ordained for you! So your biggest achievement in life shouldn't be "getting" a man. Because if you learn to wait on God, He has who He's purposed already assembled just for you! Single ladies, your value does not increase because you have a man nor does it decrease. You must know your worth and base your expectations upon that factor. When you respect your gift, you will know that not just any old body is entitled to unwrap it! Don't be so busy looking and getting... the God-sent man can't FINDETH you!!

Don't Rush

To Date or Not to Date

Okay, my sisters, I have heard many of you say that you are scared to date due to the scarcity of heterosexual men. I agree with many of you as it relates to the climate of the dating scene. Throughout the history of the "church," many of us fell into the ideals of our parents, grandparents, and elders marrying spouses who we were clearly unequally yoked with. The word declares in 2 Corinthians 6:14 to not be unequally yoked together with unbelievers. Ladies, please know that just because "he's" in church, and he may even attend faithfully and hold a title in the church doesn't mean he's the right one. A union with him can still be an unequal yoke.

Many of these churches that arrange dysfunctional relationships have contributed to the divorce rate. God's plan is always better than anything we could ever plan for ourselves. This passage of scripture doesn't place the conditions that a person will change. Yes, God does have the power to change any person, place, or thing. In 1 Corinthians 7:16, the scripture presents an open-ended question. "How do you know, wife, whether you will save your husband? Or, how do you know, husband, whether you will save your wife?"

Now, most will use both of these scriptures to refute, validate, and justify an afterthought of remaining in a dysfunctional marriage that was unequally yoked from the start. These scriptures actually are a before-thought, before entering into a vow or covenant with an unbeliever. Once you decide to step outside of the will of God, note that you shouldn't use this as a ground for divorce; in what was a willful union on your part. True obedience to God can be difficult, but it always proves worth it. Often, we rush into too many relationships in fear of losing out on having a man that, in the end, proves to create many of the strongholds that many of you are still wrestling with today. For many of you, it's almost like a game race to get the man. Please allow God the right to do His job. Allow God to develop, to groom, to prune the right mate for you. I am a firm believer and I stand by my belief that women should not be out there just running around trying to find a man. I do not believe that a woman should have to settle for any man that smiles or grins her way. Settle because a man has acquired this or that or, worse, settle for one who doesn't have any ambitions, goals, other than trying to find a woman who will take care of him.

I understand that the dating pools are slim with qualified, educated, heterosexual, driven, God-fearing, Christian men; however, this is still not to be used as an excuse to be loose and make poor choices on your selections to date. I do believe that God can show you whom He has called you to, whom He has assigned you to, as it relates to your spouse. Many of you may need to stop entertaining some of these reality television shows and social media so that you can learn to hear from God. Seek God for your mate, not your parents, your family members, coworkers, or these social media sites.

It's sad and I pray daily for women who have associated and assessed their value by being entangled with a man. Please do not minimize your worth, know that you are so much more even as a wife, as a mother, as a single woman, and, yes, even a single mother. I know many cases that these men have regrettably married out of obligation and not out of the need to "hide" behind the many masks that are worn on a weekly fellowship basis. Women, I know many in the church will say, "Well, he was raised around a lot of women"; "he adores his mother"; etc. Yes, both of these statements may be true; however, just make sure that no matter how a man's mannerisms appear, try to know his gender and sexual orientation preference. These two factors can be a key component in deciding to marry a man who is honest with you. You must be able to handle the truth.

I know many women would struggle with the thought of not only worrying about a spouse's infidelity with other women, but if you have a spouse that has a homosexual and/or bisexual past, you will also have to ensure that you can deal with infidelity with both women and men. I think a lot of the dysfunction in relationships goes overlooked before the saying of the vows. If you have questions such as these, please ask before you take vows. There are many reading this book now thinking about this in hindsight because they have married and had children by and now divorced and this has caused them to become bitter. So, if the infidelity committed was only with women, would that change your mind set on dating?

Well, there are many of you as well who have become bitter because of an estranged spouse, ex-boyfriend's infidelity with other women, and you question if you should date or not. My honest opinion is that if you know that you have allowed the bitter seeds of jealousy, mistrust, critical, cynicism, anger, and suspicion to take root in your life and these spirits are in live operation in your life, you need time to heal, you may even need deliverance. Many of us women have been taught or it's been embedded into our psyche "that a man is always going to be a man" almost as if it's alright for a man to be unfaithful, and we are to accept this behavior. I say to each his own, but we know that many of our elders, mothers, and grandmothers have been in relationships in which they were the only ones who were committed. These relationships many will say "well, they made it work" and often this is because many of those women were taught the same and felt as though they themselves were nothing without a man as well.

It is time to release and be free from those generational strongholds. This is bondage!! Many of you do not see that this has affected you rather consciously or subconsciously and may be a reason why you are attracted, or attracting, to dysfunctional men. If you have been in several relationships and the basis for all of them has pretty much been the same, the foundations of these relationships have been similar, the plots, the structures of all of your relationships have been the same, then the issue is clearly not just on these men. It is time to do a self-evaluation of yourself. The common numerator or denominator, no matter how you slice it, sweetheart, it's you. Why do you choose the same type of men? Or why have you chosen the same type and now you are convinced about settling? To date or not date is the question you should be pondering on.

Many of you are willing to settle for ex-rapists, drug users, abusers, manipulators, swindlers, and pedophiles. My plea to those of you who are not actively involved in church is to seek someone who can give you spiritual enlightenment. Seek someone who has wisdom, love, discernment, and compassion who will not only listen to you, but also advise you. It is always best to seek one who may not be familiar with you, because someone who knows you may feel compelled to be more concerned about your feelings versus your overall wellbeing. Please take the next page to journal some thoughts on where you see yourself in 5 years for short-term goals; where you see yourself in 10 years for a long-term goal. How important is it for you to be married? What kind of mate do you need in your life that will bring glory to God? What are your personal interests? These are just a few questions that you may need to address with yourself. I love you and there is nothing you can do about it; love yourself more to require more!!

Faith in the Wait

Women, you all have discernment; many just choose not to use it. The gift of discernment is in fact a gift that the Holy Spirit gives and endows certain persons with, to clearly or candidly distinguish between influences. Are these influences of God, Satan, worldly, or carnal fleshly influences? The New Testament gives us an outline on the ability to recognize and distinguish between spirits. Reference your reading in 1 Corinthians 12:10 as well as in Hebrews 5:14.

Ladies, you must get better control over your flesh, over your loins, your beings. Also, you must get a better grasp on who you are and what you deserve. This is basically a continuation of the previous chapter as it relates to being unequally yoked from the dating phase. I do believe that the pickings are slim as it relates to the present dating culture. I must touch on the point of you women who are purposely pursuing these bisexual men to be your husband. A lot of women for the sake of being loved, and appreciated, knowingly pursue these men who are living in almost a reprobated mind state to marry and procreate with. As a woman of God who works within deliverance ministry, let me advise you: You are welcoming many perverse spirits along with additional strongholds. Most of these men in church who are struggling with their sexuality will marry you in attempts to "appear" to be manly, yet he is more feminine than you are.

Many leaders will watch, counsel, and arrange marriages to these men who clearly have an identity crisis, so how can they know their identity in Christ? Do you know who you are in Christ? It behooves me that many women, right in the church, think that they can change a man into being whom they want him to be. When your desires become the Lord's desires for your life then and only then can you expect to have a mate that's already assembled or in a condition that you have been graced with or anointed to handle. Quite frankly, all of us are not builders, all of us are not leaders, all of us are not homemakers, or caretakers, many are not nurturers, or capable providers. Where do you fit in this equation? If you are waiting on God to send you your mate, you can never go wrong; however, your wait because of your own fleshly carnal desires may seem a lot longer than your friend's or cousin's.

I know many are in different places spiritually; however, we must understand that marriage in itself is a ministry. Many are on their second, third, and possibly fourth quest to be remarried. Can you have faith in the wait? I would recommend to those who find it hard waiting while remaining consecrated to the will of God to find you a hobby. Many of you have lost your own sense of identity because you have allowed a man to illegally define you. There are many hobbies that you can research, there is certainly nothing wrong with furthering your education. Single mothers, there are so many grants and financial aids available to you, and you can channel some of that energy into empowering yourselves. If you are struggling in your state of singleness, please don't lose heart. The word declares in Psalm 37:5-7 ESV: "Commit your way to the Lord, trust also in Him, and He will do it." Wow, that verse is brief but very profound in nature. The NET Bible with the same verse states: "Commit your future to the Lord! Trust in him, and he will act on your behalf."

Many women place their happiness and joy in all the lovers, boyfriends, or mates they acquire. Psychologically and emotionally, their moods resemble that of one who may suffer from depression and mood swings due to these factors being contingent upon the status and what may be the present condition of their relationship. When you don't trust God, and you choose to date someone whom you know is unequally yoked, you are apt to live unholy and impure lifestyles. It's important that not just within dating but in all things God's timing is most definitely not our timing. You may have to seek God and truly repent and ask of Him to change your desires. Many do not think there is a possibility of being happy within singleness. The truth of the matter is that many of you need to embrace singleness; to allow yourself time to heal, to focus, to allow God to pour more into you spiritually. When you begin to understand that marriage is indeed a ministry, you will be more careful to ensure that you don't entertain unfruitful connections, only what's purposeful for your purpose!

Can you have faith in the wait, and I know many can make it seem like an easy task and there will be times of loneliness, but it should never get so severe that you find yourself pursuing and making demonic soul-ties? God's plans for our lives may even differ of course from what we feel that we should have. When you embrace that God's will is what's best for you, then you will be able to overcome the shadow of doubt, fear, and loneliness. It's always a process on the road to the promise.

Kill, Steal, and Destroy

Walk in Authority

We all know that the enemy comes merely to kill, steal, and destroy. The enemy wants to kill your purpose, kill your dreams, and kill your healthy mental, physical, spiritual, and emotional capacity. The enemy wants to steal your joy, peace, purpose, dreams, and goals. Lastly, but surely not the least, the enemy seeks to destroy your character, name, image, and mental, emotional, spiritual and physical stability.

Whenever the enemy can attack you mentally, this will be the gateway to all areas within you and how you adapt and/or adopt a different perspective to your surroundings, environment, and the people whom exist closely or unknowingly alongside you. Has a series of poor relationships, one after the next, made you start second-guessing or questioning if God, in fact, has a God-ordained spouse for you? Did your poor image of relationships stem from your parents not remaining together or in fact unfaithful grandparents? Did the poor portrayal of what a relationship was played out by you yourself being involved in an abusive relationship? Have you allowed yourself to be a partaker in dysfunction while your children have bared witness of this fact? Strongholds must be broken, to ensure that a generational curse stops right at you and does not go any further than you. You must get free to ensure your family remains free. It comes first with you mentally accepting and identifying where the issue lies as it relates to an unhealthy mindset. It is time that you begin to walk in your God-given authority and begin, as Romans 4:17 declares, "to call those things that are not as though they were." We must embrace this authority as mothers especially those who have found themselves single-parenting. If there was any dysfunction within the other parent and/or yourself, denounce these spirits; kill these spirits and unhealthy mindsets in the name of Jesus.

Boundaries

Status Changes

Wow, how many times have you seen on Facebook people's personal relationship statuses change? They go from single, to in a relationship, engaged, back to single, in addition to married and/or divorced. I've never understood how several Facebook friends' status changes more frequently than others, but anyhow that's another topic for another day. The status changes not only make an impact within a national book, but also your personal life. Mothers, you must be careful to establish boundaries long before you get back on the dating scene, and surely before you get into a relationship. What do you know about this dude? Where is he from? Who are his parents/siblings? Does he have children/ex-wife/estranged spouse? I probe these questions because many of you have allowed men into your lives, whom you know limited or no information and history about. These are the men whom you have not established, nor set any boundaries before you decided to allow him to cohabitate and co-parent with you.

First things first, you should never give a man permission to discipline your kids if he has no or little involvement with his own children. You should never give permission to a man to discipline your children if he has some kind of addiction or has been incarcerated for anything involving a child. Many of you are connecting with men who are pedophiles or have some kind of falsehood of healthy sexual interactions or intimacy. You should never allow a man to interact with your children on a one-on-one basis if you don't know all the factors about him. Do your research, ladies; if not for you, do it for your children. I just don't know any love other than the love of Christ that can possibly love you the way you need to be loved. Do not forfeit this for the sake of having some biceps and thighs lying next to you. No man should be able to destroy your ministry to your children.

Ladies, I cannot stress the importance of seeking God wholeheartedly; expect God to speak to you concerning your desires in a mate. I have never seen a person who just assumes because a man attends church makes him the perfect mate. This is surely a misconception. So with that said, don't allow church folks to try to hook you up with a brother so and so and yet nobody can discern that this man has a perverse and abusive spirit. You get with this man and all hell breaks loose in your home with your children. Most people will tell you, "Well, your kids just don't want you to be anyone." This may be true to a certain extent; however, children can be brutally honest and can see things that as an adult we refuse to acknowledge. It's not that your children may be acting disrespectful towards whom you've chosen, the fact is that this man is not any good for you or them.

Some may disagree with me as it relates to the importance of your children liking or being accepting of your mate. My response is, you are entitled to your opinion. A stranger will never be able to have more influence upon my decisions than those that I've birthed. Yes, the power of influence many children shut down on their mothers after accepting a mate who is worse than their own father. Imagine how they would feel because the truth of the matter is that many of you women tolerate more poor behaviors and habits from new boyfriends and/or spouses than you were willing to accept from the man whom you've procreated with. Yes, I know there's a song and story that can fit just about any situation. However, the thing is, we must be careful to not impose our own personal views of a mate upon our children and not per se hear how they feel about your choice in a mate.

Many of you negate your children's feelings and thoughts regarding your selection in partners. For the sake of your salvation and to prevent destroying your relationship with your children, please stop being careless with your heart. Every man cheesing and grinning in your face or in your direction, sweetheart, has not been sent by God. Please stop hooking up with random men and for God's sake stop inviting these men into your home where not only you reside, but also where your children also reside. Set boundaries, ladies, the territory which you share with your children should be regarded and protected by any means necessary and at all costs. Seek God about healthy boundaries that should be intact long before you decide to get involved.

Lastly, please stop entering multiple relationships with the same mindset that it may not work out!! You can't continue to bring different men in and out of your life without bringing them in and out of your children's lives. REMEMBER that!! I am a firm believer a mother forms the first ideas or precepts of either a healthy or unhealthy relationship with their child. They judge every one of their relationships and/or experiences based upon this or the lack of this. It's ok to have healthy boundaries that need not be compromised. Healthy boundaries are good for everyone.

Consecration

Mind, Body, and Soul

Many churches have a yearly observance time of consecration. Consecration is a religious dedication of purpose or service. As single mothers, I do think that it is important that you understand that some things should be admonished and recognized as sacred. Your mind, body, and soul must be consecrated unto God due to the nature of our heart, will, and emotions; so yes, FLESH must die! We often find ourselves in and out of unhealthy connections and relationships that the voice of the enemy seems to appear stronger than the voice of the Holy Spirit. If you are not familiar with hearing the voice of the Holy Spirit, then you may have found yourself being led astray more so than others. If there is a nagging in your spirit, a feeling of unrest that doesn't sit well with your spirit this often gets mistaken as not being the HOLY SPIRIT. We must know how to distinguish between the two.

Many times, what appears to be not of God is because we allow our flesh, our will, and our emotions get in the way. The Holy Spirit will always tell you to do what's right, let me make that clear. The human element within any of us will surely fail every time if it had not been for God's saving grace and His mercy. How does one consecrate their mind, body, and soul, you may ask? Well, let's just make this plain and clear. I know abstaining from sex seems to be almost like a foreign language or an undefined tongue spoken even in the church today. Nobody wants to deal and tackle this issue because of the free grace messages being handed down. True, we need God's grace; however, abstaining from premarital sex would definitely limit the times of abusing this right. Premarital sex can have your mind, body, and soul under the direct arrest of the enemy. This is a direct scheme from the enemy to keep you in bondage; to place a stronghold upon you because of whatever issues may have already been a foothold within your bloodline.

Consecrate yourself! Another way you can consecrate your mind, body, and soul is to know and identify your very own weaknesses. If you know that being around the opposite sex in close quarters, such as house gatherings, restaurants, lounges etc. tempts you, then you should not be in attendance. Consecrate yourself! If you have a high sex drive or have found yourself with the GHAMS (Gotta Have A Man Syndrome), then your temptation level and decision-making skills will always be tested and come under fire because of the burning in your loins. Consecrate yourself. If this describes you and your nature, then you may need to speak over your life daily: "DIE FLESH!"

As a mother, it is important that your children see and witness you exercise self-control. You clearly are not using good judgment when you exempt yourself from the same measure you are extending even in the role of mother. It doesn't make it right because you say it; it becomes evident when you live it. In the Bible, the word "consecration" implies sanctification, to be pure, to be holy. Being consecrated to God and in our relationship with Him will surely aid in us in keeping true to biblical principles. The bible denotes in 2 Corinthians 6:17: "Therefore come out from among them and be separate says the Lord. Touch no unclean thing, and I will receive you." If we are to offer our bodies as a living sacrifice unto God, as Paul instructs us in Romans 12:1, then we must also ask ourselves the questions and not omit from scripture if what we are offering God is holy and pleasing to Him. Are we fully connected to God to be consecrated unto Him? True, we can look at, over time, that auntie, that older second cousin, and, yes, even your grandma may have portrayed a consecrated lifestyle and yet still battled with those "closet" demons. Demons don't discriminate. Many of our pioneer mothers were challenged and battled with many of the same demons you face today.

Holiness and sanctification are about being clean from the inside out, not from the outside in. It has been acceptable with pretending in our Christian lives, which makes it even more difficult to be fully consecrated unto God. Our conviction should also lead us to living a consecrated life as it relates to our relationship with God. As mothers, it is important that if you have been living in opposition to what you have preaching, your children may not embrace the new you, the delivered you now. It is important that you consecrate your relationship with your children and place those hurts, the misunderstandings under the feet of Jesus. The Word declares in Ephesians 1:22-23: "And God placed all things under his feet and appointed him to be head over everything for the church, which is the body, the fullness of him who fills everything in every way." Put Jesus on it and put it under His feet. It's time to walk in your freedom. It is time to give all matters of the heart over to Jesus and to live a consecrated life unto God. He is able to do what seems and what appears to be impossible. You can be cleaned from the inside out. Turn your heart and your life over to God. Don't allow anyone to speak over you or your children, "You're going to be just like such and such." The devil is the father of lies, so do not accept this over you. You can be happy in mind, body, and soul~ wholeness and holiness.

Love Is a Battlefield

There's a War Going On!

The mental and emotional games that the enemy tries to invoke, provoke, and evoke upon us can be very sneaky, cunning, or quite possibly familiar. Many of you have searched for years on conquering the battlefield of love versus lust; love versus pain; but ultimately, the battlefield of love versus you. Where does the single mother stand in all of this? How can I live consecrated and still long to be loved? How can I relate to other single mothers who are fine with living contrary to what the Bible says? I know it is much easier said than done, a topic that me and my dad had long ago. Is it easier to do what's right than wrong? Of course, we differed in answers, as per he said that it is easier to do what's right. So, let me raise the question amongst my readers. Is this question more complex or can you say wholeheartedly that it is easier to do what's right?

If it is easier to do right, then, as humans, why is it so much easier to fail at doing the wrong things, choosing the wrong people, saying the wrong thing, choosing the wrong path, just making the wrong decisions in life? Where do we go wrong, especially in the love department? Many single mothers, of course, didn't sign up for the role of being a single parent; with all the weight and the cares of the world accosted upon your shoulders, but meanwhile back at the ranch. Here we go life in hindsight, what made you do the things you've done when it comes to love? Are you able to say that your heart, motives, your intentions were pure? Some of you may have given birth to "get back" babies. Yes, those babies that you figured you wanted to get impregnated by that man to get back at the girl or woman he cheated on you with. Or in fact if you were the other woman and you had the seed of bitterness in you to plot the "get back" baby. Possibly, you gave birth to the "piece of me" baby, the baby or babies you thought would hold on to a man. My goodness, and just like the man in scenario 1, he too is not around.

Love has been a battlefield for many because of the standards in which you thought you had set for yourself; you basically settled. Or we have that Slick Rick fairytale of a teenage love, those in which you were too young to even know who you really were, let alone someone else. Marrying young due to the pressures of parents, and church family because it was rendered the way to right your wrong. So, there we have the "oops" babies. The war of love versus self-hate stems from many women who have been raped, molested, or suffered at the hands of abuse of a perpetrator either inside the family home or the church house. These acts commenced against you could be the reason why you have made poor choices and some poor decisions in your life. True, there are many of you reading this right now who either experienced a family secret or knows someone in the family who has had to live and some die with the family secret. There were a lot of babies born out of wrong situations but trust that God can make your wrongs right. Healing must take place; it shall take place right now in Jesus name. Love does not have to continue to be a battlefield. Allow God to have your heart.

One of my favorite scriptures is Psalm 51:10: "Create in me a clean heart, O God, and renew a right spirit within me." This plea David was making unto God was a petition to Him to create and give him a new heart, one that is pure. David's plea to renew a right spirit was his request to make him new to restore his heart and his spirit. Healing must take place in order for you to forgive yourself for making what were poor choices; those decisions that you thought were fatal were not final. You are able to love again and capable of being loved. I minister to myself with this. There have been many things that I have done, not pleasing to myself and in the eyes of man I should have been dead. But God saved me for such a time as this.

For the single mother that is beating herself up because of how she came to be a mother, forgive yourself so that you can heal, forgive the perpetrator for that act that made you a mother, forgive your children for being innocent, and ask for their forgiveness of your actions during this time. I have prided myself in raising my children that I have taught them to never take advantage of the time they have been given daily. We can get many things back, but time is not one of them. I want you to know that God can heal your heart right where you are right now. God can mend the broken pieces of your heart. Forgive the forced unhealthy relationships for those of you who married too young to know any better and received hell wishes from hell hounds about divorce. Most of those who wished hell upon you aren't living according to the Bible, not just a scripture or two. Forgive them because many of you are dealing with the results of raising children in the middle of dysfunction and abusive relationships. For those of you mothers who conceived out of wedlock one time or more, God forgives. My prayer is that you do not believe the lies of enemy or any negative self-images he may have attempted to put on you.

Allow God to change your heart, to change your perception of yourself. God offers and extends to us an agape love that cannot be compared. Trust that God also has an imperfect vessel that He has made perfectly just for you. This mate is far from being perfect, like you, but he shall complement, not complete you. Trust God in knowing that there may be a war going on, but God says the battle is not yours, it all belongs to Him. Have it in mind that you shall have the victory, even in love!! Take this time to reflect on how you can love others better and how you can love yourself better. Love on purpose; in purpose.

Healing

Downtime!

Every living creature that God has placed on this earth needs and requires a period of rest, a time of stillness, yes, downtime. This includes all mothers too. I know it seems like there are not enough hours in the day- between working fulltime on a 9 to 5; but we still must find time for downtime. Many times, some of my sisters think that the pressures and the stresses of single motherhood are too much, so they pursue relationship after relationship with no downtime in between.

Downtime is a healing time for you as well as in some cases your children. I am sure if you look back over your life, you were raised differently from some family members, friends, or even co-workers. What is the common factor as it relates to how these individuals function and, yes, even pursue relationships? I am a little old-fashioned in believing the word to be true in Proverbs 18:22: "He who finds a wife finds a good thing and obtains favor from the Lord." Downtime is necessary, ladies, because when those inner self-issues arise, that's when you really don't know who you are, then you will never know what you're entitled to. It's in the downtime when many mothers become desperate! Desperation can lead to unbeknownst thirst; to where you settle for anything (COUNTERFEIT). Be careful that your desires are what God desires for you. Out of thirst or hunger within your downtime season, your appetite can change. I must advise you, however, anytime you can't wait on God, it will make you do things that you probably wouldn't normally do just merely out of desperation. Don't allow your need for attention to drive you into another relationship of false affection. Another soul-tie created that will eventually prove to be what you settled for instead of what God graced you for.

Ironically, many of my saved sisters and church-going sisters think that downtime is somehow them being punished by God. Many of my sisters honestly do not know how to function without a man, although the ones they have previously had were not a reflection of what God created a man to be. It is the downtime which should be considered as healing time that you get quiet before God and await His direction.

Most of us have made many mistakes in the downtime because we couldn't remain still or quiet enough to hear from God and await His instructions and His direction. Healing time is necessary to purge yourselves from the past pains, the previous failed relationships. The downtime allows a time of self-reflection and observation. Unfortunately, many of my sisters will use this time to still entertain those who have been their source of hurt and abuse, just now with limited access. The Holy Spirit that lives within me will tell you that this is not what God wants for you. Single mothers consecrate your emotions; subject your flesh to the will of God. Allow this downtime to be a healing time for you and your children; while you were overextending yourself to make a relationship work that was not ordained by God in the first place, the relationship with your children did suffer a hit. Your children are your first ministry, single mother! They are the empty vessels in which you should be pouring into.

Use the downtime to find out who you are so that you can get healed for real. I encourage any of you reading this who are struggling and suffering in silence, please find a local deliverance ministry if you're at a church which is not tapped into healing and deliverance. Take the steps to you becoming whole and healed! The downtime is healing time. Look and find support groups for single mothers in your local and surrounding area. Allow the downtime to be an opportunity to enroll in school, take a sewing class, and find a class in a field of interest to invest your time and energy into. This will build your confidence up and grant you a new perspective that you are more than just having a man. Allow the downtime to be healing time to find out who you are, what you like and do not like, and the goals you have other than having a man. Do not spend another day allowing your children to associate singleness as a disease; singleness can be done healthily with God's guidance and His intervention; however, He needs access! Downtime is His healing time; rest in Him, allow Him to hide you and prepare you until He is ready to release you

Cosmetic Church Consummations

"It Just Looks Good"

I thank God for the gift of discernment, and as I get older and a lot wiser, I realize that unlike other gifts some are not filled with this gift. In 1 Corinthians 12:10 "....... to another [is given the gift of] discerning spirits."

Ladies, as we see the condition of the modern church, many of you who are yet to get married or those of you who desire to remarry are considering the thought of settling. Many of you are settling on younger men who are barely older than your very own children or the older deacons and/or elders of the church who are old enough to be your dad or grandfather. Then the option of those men whom you know are more feminine than you, yet for some strange reason, you have been blinded to the mannerisms that are so obvious to the "carnal" eye, never mind the "spiritual" eye.

The fact of the matter is that many of these men are not on the down low; your HOLY SPIRIT has not been tuned high. This comes from not allowing Him access to you. The Holy Spirit, if allowed, will give you spiritual insight, direction, and your capacity to embrace a newfound spiritual perception. The ability to discern spirits is a supernatural ability endowed within some by the Holy Spirit. In life and regarding those of you who are casually dating or dating with the intent of marrying, the apostle John records in 1 John 4:1: "Beloved, do not believe every spirit, but test [TRY] the spirits, whether they are of God; because many false prophets have gone out into the world."

Being able to spiritually see a person's spirit can save you a lot of heartache as well as time. We have too many cosmetic consummations within the church. Women who know their spouses are not heterosexual are saying I do every day. Cosmetic consummations within the church are on the rise because many of these men do not want deliverance, they are living in denial. Usually, both parties will end up just using each other for the appearance of a marriage that's unequally yoked, an illegal consummation. Ladies, before you say, "I do," if you lack this gift of discernment, please surround yourselves around those who are in tune with the Holy Spirit who may offer you some free advice beforehand.

Single and Selective

Too Much Thirst and Not Many Standards

I know many who know me think that I am very shallow or even stuck up, especially when it comes to the opposite sex that nothing really impresses me. In these days that we are living in, the church has become a cesspool of anything goes and everything goes down except living the Word of God. I am the daughter of a pastor, so trust me I've seen some things, but never seen the thirst that I have witnessed in the past several years within many ministries that consisted of the majority of these fellowships dominated primarily by single mothers. I often feel like the oddball case in point that I do not believe that any man should be able to catch your eye and/or attention just because he attends church.

I know many of you have heard the saying, "The biggest demons are right in the church." Well, what I can tell you is that this is true to a certain extent. Single mothers are making a mockery out of holiness and do not believe that God can keep them if they want to be kept. Many leaders have strayed so far away from preaching holiness because the condition of the church is that you can't be single and have standards. We have accepted and been conditioned that you aren't supposed to be selective or too picky because of you either a divorcee with children, widow with kids, or just a baby mama. Ladies, there is absolutely nothing wrong with you for waiting on God to send you your God-ordained spouse. For those of you that God has in waiting and have been preparing you for your spouse, continue to go through your Queen Esther process. I have spoken to several women and I too agree and know firsthand that when God has you in a waiting process and you know whom God had ordained for you will not be anything less than what God says you can have and that you deserve, it makes the process a lot easier.

Being selective for whom God has selected for you requires you always being surrendered to the Holy Spirit; you consecrate your flesh to God and seek only to please Him. There are way too many single mothers in the church who throw themselves at these men and then wonder why these same behaviors are being acted out and portrayed now within their children. Some ignorantly seek self-satisfaction and gratification that they lower their standards for a mate only to set higher unachievable expectations for their children.

Single mothers, within the hiding season, you will be refined. Do not be ashamed of God's pruning. Make no apologies. Quite frankly, many single mothers should welcome this process of God doing open heart surgery; stripping down their poor thinking, bad behaviors, and poor habits. Many of you opt to continuously get naked for all these men but have never come naked and surrendered to God! There's absolutely nothing wrong with having standards and not settling, and never allow anyone to tell you any different.

Be Processed

God Is Preparing You

For those of you who are not familiar with Esther in the bible and the process, I will briefly touch on some facts as it relates to the biblical account of women being prepared for their spouse. Many women who God has revealed who He has selected for you, will continue to hear negativity and the jeers of those who really lack faith. Single mothers, this is a process that should be considered, especially if you have a history of making poor selections. As we review the story of Queen Esther in Esther 2:12, we read that historically before a girl can meet with the king, King Ahasuerus (Xerxes), they had to be prepared for 12 months. Yes, twelve months, ladies; a whole calendar year. Now scripture does not go into details as to why the beauty process or purification process required this amount of time; however, it was practiced procedures that were regarded by the women in general. This could have very well been traditional views and morals passed down from grandmothers and mothers alike, nevertheless standards and morals were established. Now, mind you, those who participated in this process were selected first to go through the process. The process included six months with oil and myrrh and six with perfumes and cosmetics.

Now, single mothers, many of you have let yourselves go since your ex-husband or baby daddy; therefore, this has changed your outlook on believing that you should be happy and entertain any clown regardless of how they look. God is not going to send you someone that He knows that you will struggle with remaining faithful too. That's a different topic for a different day, back to Esther. Those who were chosen to go through the process had to be prepared. What are you avoiding in your life that has been a generational curse in your bloodline that you refuse to seek deliverance and total healing from poor relational choices? Why are you avoiding the process of being pruned, prepared, and processed? I want to encourage those of you women whom I have heard loud and clear and truly identify with you that God can keep you and He will sustain you.

Unfortunately, many who profess and confess Jesus will tell you that you are crazy for waiting and that God didn't tell you to wait. Most of you probably cannot tell even family members that God has your spouse in His preparation process along with you and when it's God's set time, He will orchestrate this. The beautifying process is necessary so that God can work on what's ugly about us from the inside out. Single mothers, you're not being picky, you're just respecting your process. Declare and decree that "I accept God's plans for me and my spouse will know how to locate me."

Deliverance and Healing

Never Alone

Deliverance and healing are two different ministries which feed, operate, are fueled, and complement each other. The presence of the Holy Spirit makes both ministries and process move mightily as in the breaking of yokes and chains and pulling people out of bondage. In the previous readings, we see how being processed and prepared is important and vital when we allow God to handle the season of singleness. Many mothers, during the season of singleness, may see many characteristics of their mothers, aunties, or grandmothers' surface and how they viewed them if they had ever seen them within a productive marriage and/or effective and encouraging family relationships. Many mothers now reflect to now, they themselves being victims of verbal, emotional, and or physical abuse from their childhood, only to be back at square one with those whom they have procreated with.

How does one break the cycle of abuse, you may ask? Again, I can advise you to seek the help of any spiritual leader, whom you trust and know that they hear from God. I know many refer you to a counselor or therapist but trust me a good spiritual leader can assist you via your process of healing and deliverance if this is something that you cannot do on your own with the help of God. We need deliverance to break the yokes of anything that we have settled for which includes being treated poorly.

We cannot control how other people treat us; however, we can control the way we feel about ourselves. Don't allow other opinions of you to restrict you, limit you, or allow you to settle for less. If this is the case-deliverance and healing are necessary. Merely coping with abuse becomes strongholds and deliverance is necessary to break the yokes that have been set forth and dispatched by the enemy to cause you to repeat this cycle or either die early as a circumstance of not dealing with what's killing you or stunting your growth and limiting your potential.

We often want to complain about singleness and the enemy knows that if God can get you alone and quiet, there are some things that He wants to reveal to you. He wants your full attention to show you YOURSELF!! The enemy knows that oftentimes it's right in the alone time that your breakthrough can happen. It is in the alone time that God can perfect some things that need to be worked on in you and with you. God is gracious, and He wants what's best for you. My heart goes out to any woman who has been faced with any abuse on any scale. I want to encourage you single mothers who are currently experiencing some form of abuse or you are going through your alone time right now. TRUST GOD!! Trust the process!

Recover and Discover

Self-Induced Deliverance

Mothers, as you reflect and possibly record events that have taken place in your life and have been awakened through your reading, let me encourage you on your way to deliverance and healing. There are some steps that you can proactively take on your way to recovery. Recover what was stolen as it relates to your happiness, self-esteem, peace, and joy. Discover who God has called you to be, and who He has purposed you to be. It's time to change our stinking thinking, behaviors, habits, and actions; however, you will first have to acknowledge that you have some areas of weaknesses. So, acknowledge and admit that you have some shortcomings that you are not pleased with.

How do your actions affect your children and those whom you have friendships and working relationships with? Do you find yourself desiring relationships like your married friends, family, coworkers, and church members? Are you obsessed with the thought of being in a relationship instead of focusing on the reasons why the other attempts failed? It is important that after you acknowledge and admit that you have some issues, you forgive yourself of all the hurt that you have allowed access to; forgive yourself for the seed of bitterness that was sown and planted in your life. Forgive yourself for not asking to be done or treated improperly. Forgive yourself for the rape, the incest, the abortion, the experimentations, the drug use, the perversion, and the mental, physical, and emotional, spiritual abuse, either self-inflicted or involuntarily you subjected yourself to.

Understand that the deliverance process may take some time. I know many want to be able to say a prayer and be done, but oftentimes deliverance will be a process. Don't get discouraged; breakthrough is possible. Sometimes it helps to write about events that have happened in your life to address those areas in which you may have suppressed as a child and long before you had your very own children. After you have acknowledged, admitted, and are working on forgiveness, make sure that you surrender yourself and all your hurts unto God. Know that Jesus has shed His blood for you and He wants you to receive freedom from anything that has held you bound. He went to the cross for us all.

Lastly, it is important that you make a conscious effort to

change your thinking, behaviors, and actions. Identify any areas that you may have damaged with your children and that needs immediate repair. Self-deliverance is possible when you're real with yourself first. When we examine Revelation 12:11, which says that we are "overcome by the blood of the Lamb and by the word of their testimony," with that said, clear the thought of your strange past off your mind. . It was necessary in order for you to help another young lady and another single mother to make it out of their dysfunction and to usher them into their deliverance and into their rightful position in Christ Jesus.

Dreams and Goals

Who Are You?

Many women do not understand how past relationships have gone astray and this is a good time to take a self-evaluation. Many of you mothers do not understand that you are a gift to any man. The word says a man doesn't receive favor from the Lord until he finds a wife (Proverbs 18:22). The word goes so far as to say that a man who finds a wife finds a treasure. How awesome would it be if all women saw themselves as a treasure? Who are you outside of having a man? What interests do you have? Many of you struggle with this thought because every woman you are related too has always based their importance off of being with a man. Most of these men were lowdown and trifling, but the body heat produced in the bed was the only requirement of your very own "uncle so and so," mama's boyfriends, mama's ex-husbands, grandma's live-ins aunt's fly-by-nights. Father help your daughters.

I solicit your efforts in finding out who you are as a person, other than being a mother, other than being a partner, other than being someone's downtime. Who are you? What would you like to accomplish in your very own life? It saddens me that many of you have associated your happiness and your very existence with being with someone. I am not in no way refuting that people want to be loved, but if you don't love yourself, how can you expect anyone else to love you. You cannot love these men more than you love your children, but most importantly you can't love any man more than you love yourself. Firstly, every man you meet is not worthy to know you intimately, let alone meet your children. Knowing who you are will make the difference in what you will tolerate and settle for. The more you care about yourself, the less you'll tolerate anyone who treats you like an option. What are your goals and dreams? What are your future aspirations in life?

Many men can see who you are in your current condition and see you as prey. Of course, you're looking for a relationship or husband; however, he's merely looking for an opportunity. You can no longer continue to invest and continue to pour into unauthorized contaminated vessels. Many of you mothers are finding out that you are these men's means of stability; you provide food, shelter, clothing, transportation, etc. How can you not read between these lines? Single mothers, it's really time that you weighed the pros and the cons of your mental and emotional unstableness. You may not think that there is anything wrong with what you are doing; however, your children are the eyes that are watching everything you do; other than their eyes, God sees you too!

Consecration

Close Your Legs, Open Your Ears

The word "consecration" is like a curse word to the so-called saints. Lord, please help your daughters! So, let me break this word down for both my church sisters and around-the-way sisters equally. The word "consecrate" in laymen's terms simply means to "set apart." How are you to do that as a single mother, you may ask?

Earlier, I stated that I have a hard time giving advice to those of you women who insist on lying with the father of your children who does not provide for his kids. How do you consecrate yourself from the ex-husband who was not the father of your children, but he helped financially in the household; however, he abused your kids? Why are you still seeing this character? How do you set yourself apart from the man who fathered your child born hooked on drugs and he was responsible for your drug habits? You have to learn to set yourself apart from these types of people, and relationships. Why are you seeking to go back; why are you seeking to be drawn back in these types of unhealthy relationships? These have nothing to offer you but a temporary "fix." These types of persons rely upon you needing them sexually, romantically, and even financially until you are taking yourself further and further out of the will of God. Simply put, you set yourself apart and consecrate yourself by doing the opposite of what's pleasing to your flesh.

Put the men down, out the habits down, and open your ears to the Holy Spirit. I just have to keep it 100 with you single mothers: close your legs and open up your bibles; wait to hear from God regarding your situation, regarding your life. God is a provider Who can meet your needs. Allow God to clean you up on the inside; allow Him to cleanse and purge anything that's not like Him out of you.

Consecration is the first step through fasting and praying that you can become more in tune with God and hear clearly the path in which He wants you to take. Sometimes the stillness of consecration will awaken dreams and visions that have been lying dormant inside of you. Consecration is not a curse word; it is a keyword, a focus word, that can assist on this journey of single parenthood. Consecrate yourself, ladies, so that your God-ordained spouse can find you. There have been too many counterfeits to come along your way, so if you're unsure of your next move, if you are unsure of establishing a better relationship with God and your children, I would suggest consecrating yourselves.

Fasting and Praying

New Beginnings

Single mothers, I would like to provide you some information regarding fasting and praying. As of recently, I have learned that not many people know what fasting and praying is all about, even those who have been in church all their lives. In the Bible, there are numerous amounts of scriptures about fasting and praying. However, to break yokes and strongholds, it is important to know that some breakthroughs are tied to the obedience of fasting and praying. Please see Matthew 17:21. It reads in King James Version: "Howbeit this kind goeth not out but by prayer and fasting." Godly women such as Anna in the Bible gave themselves to fasting and praying.

Mothers, we have been given a godly mandate to nurture and

a strong impact on the development of our children's character. I recommend any mother reading my book, if you do not have a church affiliation, please seek the Lord about placing you where you need to be as it relates to service and fellowship. Surround yourself with those who want to see the best happen for you and in you. Connect with those single mothers who have and are defying the odds. All things are possible with God (Matthew 19:26). Let me challenge you, mothers, to look into fasting. There are various types of fasting, just ensure that you are led by the Holy Spirit, and for those of you who have existing health issues please see your physician.

Saved

What Must I Do?

I would be remiss as a minister of the gospel to not extend an open invitation to accept Jesus as your Lord and Savior Jesus Christ. Please know that Jesus came so that we might have life and have it more abundantly. Do not fall into the mindset that what you've done or didn't do to become and/or warrant being a single mother has no weighing on God's love for you. God's love is unconditional! His mercies are brand new every day. There is no sin too big for God to handle, so cast all your cares upon Him. If you have tried everything else, I pray that this book opens your heart to receive Jesus today, as tomorrow may be too late.

Please see:

Acts 16:30

Acts 2:38

Romans 10:9-10

About the Author

Evonn is a proud mother of three: two sons and one daughter. An evangelist of the Gospel of Jesus Christ, Evonn has a heart for single mothers and teenage girls. She's currently working on her nonprofit business endeavors named The Latter Rain Project and Sister Keeper Ministries, and she plans to use these platforms to empower single mothers abroad.

She lives by the motto: *Your Latter Shall Be Greater!!* Evonn is a mother, minister, writer, and motivational speaker who has a heart for the ministry of single mothers, from all socioeconomic backgrounds. She has successfully obtained two degrees while being a divorced single mother and prides herself on encouraging others to do the same.

She is currently pursuing other educational goals and aspirations as she seeks to always maintain a teachable spirit. Her prayer is to operate in full-time ministry to assist mothers and teenage girls to tap into their God-given and God-ordained purpose. To foster this growth through God's biblical principles while encouraging and building everyday life achievements.

No matter your circumstance, be it divorced, widowed, or an ex-anything, she is a living witness that you can be free to blossom into your God-purposed identity: **From Broken to Blessed** and **From Pain to Purpose!**

For more information and speaking engagements:

The Latter Rain Movement

www.thelatterrainmovement@gmail.com

Bibles and Baskets Outreach Ministry